STUDY GUIDE

Charles Beem
Bucks County Community College

Danica Lavoie
Centennial College

MARKETING
Real People, Real Decisions

Updated First Canadian Edition

Michael R. Solomon
Elnora W. Stuart
Auleen Carson
J. Brock Smith

Prentice Hall
Toronto

0-13-046087-7

Acquisitions Editor: Kelly Torrance
Developmental Editor: Paul Donnelly
Production Editor: Mary Ann McCutcheon
Production Coordinator: Andrea Falkenberg

1 2 3 4 5   07 06 05 04 03

Printed and bound in Canada

Table of Contents

Preface

Chapter 1   Welcome to the World of Marketing 1

Chapter 2   Strategic Planning: Making Choices in a Dynamic Environment 14

Chapter 3   Decision Making in the New Era of Marketing:

Enriching the Marketing Environment 27

Chapter 4   Think Globally and Act Locally: Marketing in a Multinational

Environment 41

Chapter 5   Marketing Information and Research:

Analyzing the Business Environment..54

Chapter 6   Why People Buy: Consumer Behaviour 65

Chapter 7   Why Organizations Buy: Business-To-Business

Markets 77

Chapter 8   Sharpening the Focus:

Target Marketing Strategies...90

Chapter 9   Creating the Product 102

Chapter 10   Managing the Product..115

Chapter 11   Broadening the Product Focus:

Marketing Intangibles and Services 127

Chapter 12   Pricing the Product 139

Chapter 13   Pricing Methods 150

Chapter 14   Channel Management, Wholesaling, and Physical Distribution:

Delivering the Product 162

Chapter 15   Retailing and E-Tailing..175

Chapter 16   Integrated Marketing Communications and

Relationship Management 188

Chapter 17   Advertising..200

Chapter 18   Sales Promotion, Public Relations, and Personal Selling 212

To the Student

The purpose of this study guide is to assist you in more effectively learning the material in *Marketing: Real People, Real Decisions* by Solomon, Stuart, Carson, and Smith.

This study guide is designed and written to reinforce your learning from the textbook, class, lectures, and class discussions. The objectives of this study guide are:

1.   To provide you with the materials that will be useful in learning the business vocabulary and business concepts presented in your text.

2.   To provide you with an opportunity to test your understanding of what you have read, studies, and learned.

3.   To help you prepare for quizzes and examinations by testing yourself with sample exam-type questions.

4.   To encourage you to apply your understanding of the business concepts presented in the text to interesting, real-world business problems and opportunities.

The Organization of the Study Guide

Each chapter in this Study Guide is arranged in the following order:

1. **Chapter Overview**: The short chapter summary will help you to review the most important elements of each chapter.

2. **Learning Objectives**: The learning objectives are listed (as they appear in the beginning of each text chapter) to remind you of what you need to know once you have completed a review of the chapter.

3. **Chapter Outline**: The chapter outline requires you to define, list or describe the business concepts as they relate to each heading in the outline. The textbook page numbers are provided in order to help guide you through this learning exercise.

4. **Key Terms**: This practice exercise will allow you to test your knowledge of some of the important terms provided in each chapter.

5. **Multiple Choice**: The Multiple Choice questions were written and designed to measure your understanding of the chapter and to prepare you for course tests and exams.

6. **Chapter In Review—Writing To Learn**: This exercise provides an excellent opportunity for you to practice and develop your writing skills, while reviewing what you have learned. Enjoy the challenge as you build your confidence.

7. **Case Analysis**: Read the three-part Vignette presented in each chapter of your textbook. Apply what you have learned in reading and studying the chapter to answer the questions provided.

8. **Scenario**: Each scenario puts you in the "driver's seat". The questions following each scenario ask what you would do if confronted with a particular marketing situation, and/or require you to apply the marketing concepts you learned in the chapter.

9. **Answers**: Answers are provided for each learning exercise, with the exception of the scenario.

Special Acknowledgements

I would like to begin by thanking Don Hull, Senior Editor at Prentice Hall for allowing me the privilege to contribute my work in preparing this Study Guide to accompany the very excellent textbook, Marketing, by Solomon and Stuart. I am also grateful to John Larkin, Assistant Editor, Business, of Prentice Hall for the many useful suggestions provided to me while working on this Study Guide. Others I wish to thank include my wonderful wife, Karen, and my father, John R. Beem, M.D., who has guided and inspired me to pursue my career in teaching.

This Study Guide is dedicated to my loving wife, Karen, for her support and understanding.

Good Luck!

Charles W. Beem
Bucks County Community College
Newtown, Pennsylvania
(215) 968-8237

I would like to thank Susan Erickson, Kelly Torrance, and Michael Young of Pearson Education Canada for providing me with the opportunity to contribute to this Study Guide, and Paul Donnelly of Pearson Education Canada for his excellent guidance. I also wish to thank my husband, Martin Durand, for his unwavering support throughout this project. Finally, I wish to thank my wonderful marketing students at Centennial College, who make teaching so much fun!

Danica Lavoie
Centennial College
Scarborough, Ontario, Canada
(416) 289-5000
dlavoie@centennialcollege.ca

CHAPTER 1

Welcome to the World of Marketing

CHAPTER OVERVIEW

In this chapter, we introduced marketing as the process of planning and executing the conception, pricing, promotion, and distribution of ideas, goods, and services to create exchanges that satisfy individual and organizational objectives.

We then examined the marketing mix, tools used to create the desired response from consumer and business markets. The four tools are product, price, place, and promotion. Marketers design the marketing mix such that consumers and business consumers will seek to exchange or trade money or something else of value for the product.

The strategic process of marketing planning begins with an assessment of factors within the organization and in the external environment that will help or hinder the development and marketing of products. Based on this analysis, marketing objectives are set and strategies are developed.

Next, we explored the evolution of the marketing concept. Early in this century, companies followed a product orientation, which later evolved into a sales orientation, then a consumer orientation (which, in turn, led to the widespread adoption of the marketing concept). Today, many firms are moving toward a New Era orientation that includes not only a commitment to quality, but also a concern for both economic and social profit.

We also discovered how the marketing system is important to individual and business customers in the marketplace, in our daily lives, and in society. We considered the concept of utility—that is, the usefulness or benefit provided by a product. Four kinds of utility in marketing are form utility, place utility, time utility, and possession utility. We also examined the concept of value, including functional value, experiential value, symbolic or expressive value, and cost or sacrifice value.

Finally we explained marketing's role within an organization. Marketing decisions cannot be made in isolation from an organization's other operations; marketing, finance, manufacturing, research and development, and other functional areas must work together to achieve the organization's goals.

CHAPTER OBJECTIVES

1. Define the marketing concept.

2. Define the objectives of marketing.

3. Describe the marketing mix.

4. Understand the basics of marketing planning.

5. Describe the evolution of the marketing concept.

6. Explain how marketing is important to both individual and business customers in the marketplace, in our daily lives, and in society.

7. Explain marketing's role within an organization.

CHAPTER OUTLINE

With reference to the textbook, please provide a brief description of each of the main elements listed in the Chapter Outline below. The page numbers will help guide you through the learning process.

I.   WHAT IS MARKETING?
     Marketing_____ *(p.5)*
     A.   Marketing Satisfies Needs_____ *(p.5)*
          Consumer_____ *(p.5)*
          1.   The Marketing Concept_____ *(p.5)*
               Need _____ *(p.5)*
               Want _____ *(p.5)*
               Benefit_____ *(p.5)*
               Demand_____ *(p.6)*
               Market_____ *(p.6)*
               Marketplace_____ *(p.6)*
          2.   Satisfying Society's Needs, Too
               Social Marketing Concept_____ *(p.6)*

     B.   Marketing Is an Exchange of Value _____ *(p.7)*
          Exchange _____ *(p.7)*
          Customer Value _____ *(p.7)*

C.   (Almost) Anything Can Be Marketed
Product _____ *(p.7)*
    1.   Not-for-Profit Marketing_____ *(p.7)*
    2.   Idea, Place and People Marketing_____ *(p.8)*
    3.   Marketing Sports, Entertainment, and Places _____ *(p.8)*

D.   Marketing's Tools: The Marketing Mix _____ *(p.13)*
    1.   Product _____ *(p.13)*
    2.   Price _____ *(p.14)*
    3.   Place _____ *(p.14)*
    4.   Promotion _____ *(p.14)*

E.   Marketing as a Process _____ *(p.15)*
Relationship Marketing _____ *(p.15)*

II.   HOW ARE MARKETING DECISIONS MADE? _____ *(p.9)*
    A.   Marketing Planning _____ *(p.10)*
    Mass Market _____ *(p.12)*

    B.   Finding and Reaching a Target Market
    Market Segment_____ *(p.10)*
    Target Market _____ *(p.11)*
    1.   Segmenting the Market _____ *(p.12)*
    2.   Selecting a Target Market _____ *(p.12)*
    3.   Positioning the Product _____ *(p.13)*

III.   WHEN DID MARKETING BEGIN? THE EVOLUTION OF A CONCEPT
    A.   The Product Orientation _____ *(p.15)*

    B.   The Selling Orientation _____ *(p.15)*

    C.   The Consumer Orientation _____ *(p.16)*

    D.   The New Era Orientation _____ *(p.17)*

IV.   WHY IS MARKETING IMPORTANT? _____ *(p.17)*
    A.   Marketing Creates Value
    Functional Value _____ *(p.17)*
    Utility_____ *(p.17)*
    Form Utility _____ *(p.17)*
    Place Utility _____ *(p.17)*
    Time Utility _____ *(p.18)*
    Possession Utility _____ *(p.18)*
    Experiential Value _____ *(p.18)*
    Symbolic/Expressive Value_____ *(p.18)*
    Cost/Sacrifice Value _____ *(p.18)*

B.   Marketing's Role in the Firm _____   *(p.18)*

C.   Marketing's Role in Our Daily Lives: Opera to Oprah
        1.   Popular Culture _____   *(p.19)*
        2.   Marketing and Myths _____   *(p.19)*

D.   Marketing's Role in Society _____   *(p.19)*
        1.   Ethical Behaviour in Good Business_____   *(p.20)*
        2.   Social and Ethical Criticisms of Marketing _____   *(p.20)*

KEY TERMS

Select the correct term for each definition and write it in the space provided.

Benefit
Consumer orientation
Want
Market
Consumer
Relationship marketing
Marketing concept
Utility

Demand
Marketing
Popular Culture
Target Market
Need
Product
Mass market

1. _____   The process of planning and executing the conception, pricing, promotion, and distribution of ideas goods, and services to create exchanges that satisfy individual organizational objectives. *(p.5)*

2. _____   The ultimate user of a purchased good or service. *(p.5)*

3. _____   A management orientation that focuses on achieving organizational objectives by understanding consumer needs and wants and the associated costs of satisfying them. *(p.5)*

4. _____   Recognition of any difference between a consumer's actual state and some ideal or desired state. *(p.5)*

5. _____   The desire to satisfy needs in specific ways that are culturally and socially influenced. *(p.5)*

6. _____   Customers' desire for products coupled with the resources to obtain them. *(p.6)*

4

7. _____ The outcome sought by a customer that motivates buying behaviour. *(p.6)*

8. _____ All of the customers and potential customers who share a common need that can be satisfied by a specific product, who have the resources to exchange for it, who are willing to make the exchange, and who have the authority to make the exchange. *(p.6)*

9. _____ A tangible good, a service, an idea, or some combination of these that, through the exchange process, satisfies consumer or business customer needs; a bundle of attributes including features, functions, benefits, and uses. *(p.7)*

10. _____ A marketing philosophy that focuses on building long-term relationships with customers, suppliers, distributors, and other key stakeholders to satisfy mutual needs. *(p.15)*

11. _____ All possible customers in a market, regardless of the differences in their specific needs and wants. *(p.12)*

12. _____ The market segment(s) on which an organization focuses its marketing plan and toward which it directs its marketing efforts. *(p.11)*

13. _____ A management philosophy that focuses on being proactive and responsive in identifying and satisfying consumer needs and wants. *(p.16)*

14. _____ The usefulness or benefit received by consumers from a product. *(p.17)*

15. _____ The music, movies, sports, books, celebrities, and other forms of entertainment consumed by the mass market. *(p.19)*

MULTIPLE CHOICE

Identify the most correct answer.

1. The outcome sought by a customer that motivates buying behaviour is known as a: *(p.6)*
    a.   want.
    b.   demand.
    c.   benefit.
    d.   utility.

2. An orientation that focuses on satisfying consumer needs while also addressing the needs of the larger society is the: *(p.5)*
    a.   community marketing concept.
    b.   social marketing concept.
    c.   environmental marketing concept.
    d.   consumer marketing concept.

3. In order for an exchange to occur: *(p.7)*
    a.   at least two people or organizations must be willing to make a trade.
    b.   both parties must agree on the value of the exchange and how it will be carried out.
    c.   each party must be free to accept or reject the other's offer.
    d.   all of the above.

4. What the customer gets in the purchase, use, and ownership of a product relative to the costs and sacrifices incurred is known as: *(p.7)*
    a.   exchange.
    b.   customer value.
    c.   the marketing mix.
    d.   benefit.

5. The elements in the marketing mix are: *(p.14)*
    a.   product, price, promotion, and place.
    b.   need, product, satisfaction, and supply.
    c.   goods, service, product, and place.
    d.   planning, pricing, promotion, and distribution.

6. The seller's assignment of value to a product is the: *(p.14)*
    a.   demand.
    b.   profit.
    c.   price.
    d.   resource.

7. The availability of the product to the customer at the desired time and location is the: *(p.14)*
    a. place.
    b. resource.
    c. demand.
    d. price.

8. Promotion includes all of the communication activities undertaken to inform consumers or organizations about goods, services and ideas and to encourage them to buy, including: *(p.14)*
    a. personal selling.
    b. television advertising.
    c. store coupons.
    d. all of the above.

9. The first phase of the marketing planning process involves: *(p.10)*
    a. reaching a target market.
    b. analyzing the organization's current strengths and weaknesses.
    c. positioning the product.
    d. segmenting the market.

10. The aim of establishing a market position is to: *(p.13)*
    a. evaluate the segments identified in the segmentation process.
    b. focus on reaching as many customers as possible.
    c. determine how a product will be different and superior to competitors' products in the mind of the consumer.
    d. none of the above.

11. Management philosophy that emphasizes the most efficient ways to produce and distribute products is known as: *(p.15)*
    a. product orientation.
    b. marketing concept.
    c. product strategy.
    d. production management.

12. A seller's market is a market in which: *(p.15)*
    a. supply and demand are equal.
    b. supply is greater than demand.
    c. demand is greater than supply.
    d. none of the above.

13. New Era orientation is a: *(p.17)*
    a. management philosophy in future marketing.
    b. management philosophy in which marketing decision making means a devotion to excellence in designing and producing products and creating products that benefit the customer plus the firm's employees, shareholders, and fellow citizens.
    c. management philosophy that emphasizes aggressive sales practices and marketing is seen strictly as a sales function.
    d. management philosophy that focuses on new wave thinking.

14. The consumer benefit provided when organizations make products available where customers want them is: *(p.18)*
    a. form utility.
    b. time utility.
    c. possession utility.
    d. place utility.

15. Marketing messages that communicate stories containing symbolic elements that express the shared emotions and ideals of a culture are called: *(p.19)*
    a. myths.
    b. product essays.
    c. Morse code.
    d. artificial legends.

CHAPTER IN REVIEW—WRITING TO LEARN

1. Describe how marketers plan and develop strategies for finding and reaching a market.

_____

_____

_____

2. Explain the evolution of the marketing concept.

_____

_____

_____

3.   Explain marketing's role in the firm.

_____

_____

_____

_____

CASE ANALYSIS

Real People, Real Decisions: Meet Jacqui Cohen, Army & Navy

Reread the three sections comprising the Army & Navy vignette in Chapter 1 and answer the following questions:

1.   When Army & Navy was first launched, what was its positioning strategy?

2.   How would you describe Army & Navy's initial target market(s)?

3.   What is the main problem/opportunity facing company President Jacqui Cohen?

4.   Which of the four marketing orientations—product, selling, consumer or New Era—is evident in Army & Navy's actions? Why?

SCENARIO

Yesterday, you attended your first marketing class. You were so captivated—by the concepts, the interesting examples, the enthusiastic professor—you went straight home and read the entire first year text in one sitting. Tonight, you and your friends went out to a local restaurant and before the first course even arrived, you announced your intention to major in marketing. Your friends were outraged, and unleashed a barrage of negative comments. How do you respond to the following comments?

1.   Marketers are selling people things they don't need.
2.   Marketers are unethical. They influence children, and encourage them to ask their parents for things.
3.   Marketers are manipulative. They use images and trickery to make you buy things.
4.   Marketers are not truthful. They exaggerate the benefits of products and services.

ANSWERS

Chapter Outline

I. WHAT IS MARKETING?

Marketing—The process of planning and executing the conception, pricing, promotion, and distribution of ideas, goods, and services to create exchanges that satisfy individual and organizational objectives.

    A. Marketing Satisfies Needs—Marketing involves at least two parties—a seller and a buyer—each of whom have needs. Products are bought to satisfy consumer's needs.

    Consumer—The ultimate user of a purchased good or service.

        1. The Marketing Concept—A management orientation that focuses on achieving organizational objectives by understanding consumer needs and wants and the costs associated with satisfying them.

        Need—Recognition of any difference between a consumer's actual state and some ideal or desired state.

        Want—The desire to satisfy needs in specific ways that are culturally and socially influenced.

        Benefit—The outcome sought by a customer that motivates a buying behaviour.

        Demand—Customers' desire for products coupled with the resources to obtain them.

        Market—All of the customers and potential customers who share a common need that can be satisfied by a specific product, who have the resources to exchange for it, who are willing to make the exchange, and who have the authority to make the exchange.

        Marketplace—Any location or medium used to conduct an exchange.

        2. Satisfying Society's Needs, Too

        Social Marketing Concept—An orientation that focuses on satisfying consumer needs while also addressing the needs of a larger society.

    B. Marketing is an Exchange of Value—The buyer receives an object, service, or idea that satisfies a need, for which the seller receives something he or she feels is of equivalent value.

    Exchange—The process by which some transfer of value occurs between a buyer and a seller.

    Customer Value—What the customer gets in the purchase, use and ownership of a product relative to the costs and sacrifices incurred.

    C. (Almost) Anything Can Be Marketed.

    Product—A tangible good, a service, an idea or some combination of these that, through the exchange process, satisfies consumer or business customer needs; a bundle of attributes including features, functions, benefits and uses

        1. Not-for-Profit Marketing—Museums, churches and even zoos are now practising the marketing concept.

        2. Idea, Place, and People Marketing—Many of the famous people that you pay to see in concerts, stadiums, movies, etc. have been successfully marketed.

        3. Marketing Sports, Entertainment, and Places—Sports and entertainment activities do not just happen; they must be carefully planned. Places can also be marketed.

D. Marketing's Tools: The Marketing Mix—Consisting of the factors that can be manipulated and used together to create a desired response in the marketplace.
1. Product—A tangible good, a service, an idea, or some combination of these that, through the exchange process, satisfies consumer or business customer needs; a bundle of attributes including features, functions, benefits and uses.
2. Price—The seller's assignment of value to a product.
3. Place—The availability of the product to the customer at the desired time and location (channels of distribution)
4. Promotion—the communication activities undertaken to inform consumers or organizations about goods, services or ideas, and to encourage potential customers to buy these goods, services or ideas,

E. Marketing is a Process—It involves a series of steps that entail both careful thought (planning) and action (executing).
Relationship Marketing—A marketing philosophy that focuses on building long-term relationships with customers, suppliers, distributors and other key stakeholders to satisfy mutual needs.

II. HOW ARE MARKETING DECISIONS MADE?—Marketing is a strategic decision process, in which marketing managers determine what marketing strategies will be used to help the organization meet its long term objectives.
A. Marketing Planning—Involves analyzing the organization's current situation. Specifically this takes into account the threats and opportunities in the marketplace, actions of competitors, cultural and technological changes, the economy, etc.
Mass Market—All possible customers in a market, regardless of the differences in their specific needs and wants.

B. Finding and Reaching a Target Market
Market Segment—A distinct group of customers within a larger market who are similar to one another in some way and whose needs differ from other customers in the larger market.
Target Market—The market segment(s) on which an organization focuses its marketing plan and toward which it directs its marketing efforts.
1. Segmenting the Market—The process of dividing the overall market into segments, where the consumers in each segment have one or more important characteristics in common, setting them apart from others.
2. Selecting a Target Market—The process of evaluating the segments in terms of relative attractiveness and profitability potential against the organization's resources and ability to satisfy the needs of the segments.
3. Positioning the Product—The aim of setting a market position is to show how the product will be different and superior to competitors' products in the mind of the customer.

III. WHEN DID MARKETING BEGIN? THE EVOLUTION OF A CONCEPT
A. The Product Orientation—A management philosophy that emphasizes the most efficient ways to produce and distribute products.

B. The Selling Orientation—A management philosophy that emphasizes aggressive sales practices and marketing is seen strictly as a sales function.

C. The Consumer Orientation—A management philosophy that focuses on ways to satisfy customers' needs and wants.

D. The New Era Orientation—A management philosophy in which marketing decision making means a devotion to excellence in designing and producing products and creating products that benefit the customer plus the firm's employees, shareholders, and fellow citizens.

IV. WHY IS MARKETING IMPORTANT?
A. Marketing Creates Value
Functional Value—consumer benefits relating to product features, characteristics, utility, performance and outcomes.
Utility—The usefulness or benefit received by consumers from a product.
Form Utility—The consumer benefit provided by organizations when they change raw materials into finished products desired by consumers.
Place Utility—The consumer benefit provided when organizations make products available where and when customers want them.
Time Utility—The consumer benefit provided by storing products until they are needed by buyers.
Possession Utility—The consumer benefits provided by an organization when they allow the consumer to own, use, and/or enjoy the product.

B. Marketing's Role in the Firm—Marketing managers must work with financial and accounting officers, and people involved in manufacturing.

C. Marketing's Role in Our Daily Lives: Opera to Oprah
1. Popular Culture—The music, movies, sports, books, celebrities, and other forms of entertainment consumed by the mass market.
2. Marketing and Myths—Marketing messages often communicate myths, stories containing symbolic elements that express the shared emotions and ideals of a culture.

D. Marketing's Role in Society—We rely on marketers to sell us products that are safe and perform as promised, to tell us the truth about what they are selling, and to price and distribute these products fairly.
1. Ethical Behaviour is Good Business—Companies usually find that stressing ethics and social responsibility is also good business, at least in the long run.
2. Social and Ethical Criticisms of Marketing—Whether intentionally or not, some marketers do violate their bond of trust with consumers.

Key Terms   ## Multiple Choice

1. Marketing   1. c
2. Consumer   2. b
3. Marketing concept   3. d
4. Need   4. b
5. Want   5. a
6. Demand   6. c
7. Benefit   7. a
8. Market   8. d
9. Product   9. b
10. Relationship marketing   10. c
11. Mass market   11. a
12. Target market   12. c
13. Consumer orientation   13. b
14. Utility   14. d
15. Popular culture   15. a

Chapter in Review—Writing to Learn

1. The strategic process of marketing planning begins with an assessment of factors within the organization and in the external environment that will help or hinder the development and marketing of products. Based on this analysis, marketing objectives are set and strategies are developed. Many firms use a target marketing strategy in which the overall market is divided into segments and the most attractive is targeted. Then, the marketing mix is strategically designed to gain a competitive position in the target market.

2. Early in this century, companies followed a product orientation in which they focused on the most efficient ways to produce and distribute products. Beginning in the 1930s, some firms adopted a sales orientation that encouraged salespeople to aggressively push products on customers. In the 1950s, organizations began to adopt a consumer orientation that focused on customer satisfaction and that led to the widespread adoption of the marketing concept. Today, many firms are moving toward a New Era orientation that includes not only a commitment to quality but also concern for both economic and social profit.

3. Marketing decisions cannot be made in isolation from an organization's other operations, so marketing, finance, manufacturing, research and development, and other functional areas must work together to achieve the organization's goals.

Case Analysis

1. Army & Navy's initial market position rested on the notion of providing value to customers by purchasing merchandise from bankrupt and overstocked merchants and passing on the savings to customers.

2. Army & Navy's initial target markets were cost conscious young adults and parents with young families.

3. The main problem (or opportunity—it depends on how you look at the world!) facing Jacqui Cohen is figuring out what her target markets should be and developing a marketing strategy to reach them.

4. Army & Navy's actions suggest that the company subscribes to a consumer orientation, because the company is being proactive and responsive in identifying and satisfying consumer wants.

CHAPTER 2

Strategic Planning: Making Choices in a Dynamic Environment

CHAPTER OVERVIEW

In this chapter we learned that strategic planning by top-level managers involves defining the firm's business mission, setting corporate goals and objectives, establishing a business portfolio, and determining its strategic marketing direction. In addition, we considered how decisions about the firm's portfolio of strategic business units are often made with the help of such planning tools as the Boston Consulting Group matrix and the product-market growth matrix.

Next, we considered how firms gain a competitive advantage when they have distinctive competencies—or capabilities that are stronger than those of the competition.

The marketing planning process determines what strategies and action plans the firm will use to achieve its marketing objectives and the overall strategic goals. Marketing selects the target market(s) the organization will go after and decides what marketing strategies will be used to meet the needs of that market.

Finally, we discussed the factors involved in the implementation and control of the marketing plan, including the development of a marketing budget, the effective organization of the marketing function, and the establishment of controls in order to measure actual versus planned performance.

CHAPTER OBJECTIVES

1.   Explain the strategic planning process.

2.   Tell how firms gain a competitive advantage and describe the factors that influence marketing objectives.

3.   Describe the steps in the marketing planning process.

4.   Explain the factors involved in the implementation and control of the marketing plan.

CHAPTER OUTLINE

With reference to the textbook, please provide a brief description of each of the main elements listed in the Chapter Outline below. The page numbers will help guide you through the learning process.

I. STRATEGIC PLANNING: GUIDING THE BUSINESS
Strategic Planning _____ *(p.30)*
Tactical Planning _____ *(p.31)*
Operational Planning _____ *(p.31)*
Cross-Functional Planning_____ *(p.31)*
  A. Defining the Organization's Business Mission _____ *(p.32)*
    Mission Statement _____ *(p.32)*

  B. Evaluating the Environment: SWOT Analysis _____ *(p.34)*
    1. Internal Environment _____ *(p.34)*
    2. External Environment _____ *(p.34)*

  C. Setting Organizational Objectives _____ *(p.35)*
    Objectives _____ *(p.35)*

  D. Planning for Growth
    1. Portfolio Analysis: Strategic Business Units
      Strategic Business Units _____ *(p.35)*
      Business Portfolio _____ *(p.36)*
      Portfolio Analysis _____ *(p.36)*
    2. The Boston Consulting Group Matrix_____ *(p.36)*
      Stars_____ *(p.37)*
      Cash Cows_____ *(p.37)*
      Question Marks _____ *(p.37)*
      Dogs _____ *(p.37)*
    3. Product-Market Growth Matrix _____ *(p.38)*
      Market Penetration _____ *(p.38)*
      Market Development_____ *(p.38)*
      Product Development _____ *(p.38)*
      Diversification_____ *(p.38)*

II. THE MARKETING PLANNING PROCESS
  A. Creating a Competitive Advantage: Marketing's Strategic Focus
    Competitive Advantage_____ *(p.40)*
    1. Identifying Distinctive Competencies
      Distinctive Competency _____ *(p.40)*
    2. Providing Differential Benefits
      Differential Benefits _____ *(p.41)*

B. Setting Marketing Objectives
    1. Sales Objectives _____ *(p.42)*
    2. Product-Oriented Objectives_____ *(p.42)*
    3. Market Objectives _____ *(p.42)*

III.   DEVELOPING MARKETING STRATEGIES: ELEMENTS OF A MARKET PLAN
    A. Selecting a Target Market _____ *(p.44)*

    B. Developing Marketing Mix Programs_____ *(p.44)*
        1. Product Strategies _____ *(p.44)*
        2. Pricing Strategies _____ *(p.45)*
        3. Promotion Strategies _____ *(p.45)*
        4. Distribution Strategies_____ *(p.46)*

    C. Preparing a Marketing Plan _____ *(p.46)*
        Situation Analysis _____ *(p.46)*

IV.   IMPLEMENTATION AND CONTROL OF THE MARKETING PLAN
    A. Implementing the Marketing Plan_____ *(p.47)*
        1. The Marketing Budget _____ *(p.47)*
        2. Organizing the Marketing Function _____ *(p.48)*
    B. Controlling the Marketing Plan_____ *(p.48)*
        1. Trend Analysis _____ *(p.48)*
        2. Marketing Research _____ *(p.48)*
        3. The Marketing Audit_____ *(p.50)*

KEY TERMS

Select the correct term for each definition and write it in the space provided.

Market penetration

Control

Mission statement

Competitive advantage

Strategic planning

Market development

Objectives

Implementation

Portfolio analysis

Operational planning

Distinctive competency

Cross-functional planning

Marketing budget

Business portfolio

Marketing plan

1. _____   A managerial decision process that matches an organization's resources and capabilities to its market opportunities for long-term growth and survival. *(p.30)*

2. _____   A decision process that focuses on developing detailed plans for day-to-day activities that carry out an organization's tactical plans. *(p.31)*

3. _____   A formal statement in an organization's strategic plan that describes the overall purpose of the organization and what it intends to achieve in terms of its customers, products, and resources. *(p.32)*

4. _____   Specific goals, accomplishments, or outcomes that an organization hopes to achieve by a specific time. *(p.35)*

5. _____   The group of different products, or brands, owned by an organization and characterized by different income-generating and growth capabilities. *(p.36)*

6. _____   A management tool for evaluating a firm's business mix and assessing the potential of an organization's strategic business units. *(p.38)*

7. _____   Growth strategies designed to increase sales of existing products to current customers, non-users, and users of competitive brands in served markets. *(p.38)*

8. _____   Growth strategies that introduce existing products to new markets. *(p.38)*

9. _____   An approach to planning in which managers work together in developing tactical plans for each functional area in the firm, so that each plan considers the objectives of the other areas. *(p.31)*

10. _____   An advantage over competitors that an organization gains through its superior capabilities and unique product benefits that provide greater value in the minds of the consumer. *(p.40)*

11. _____   A superior capability of a firm in comparison to its direct competitors. *(p.40)*

12. _____   A document that describes the marketing environment, outlines the marketing objectives, and identifies who will be responsible for carrying out each part of the marketing strategy. *(p.46)*

13. _____   The stage of the strategic management process in which strategies are put into action on a day-to-day basis. *(p.47)*

14. _____   A statement of the total amount to be spent on the marketing function and the allocation of money or the spending limit for each activity under a marketer's control. *(p.47)*

15. _____   Measuring actual performance, comparing it to planned performance, and making necessary changes in plans and implementation. *(p.48)*

MULTIPLE CHOICE

Identify the most correct answer.

1. A decision process that concentrates on developing detailed plans for strategies and tactics for the short term that supports an organization's long-term strategic plan is: *(p.31)*
    a.   strategic planning.
    b.   tactical planning.
    c.   operational planning.
    d.   short-term planning.

2. In the first stage of strategic planning, a firm's top executives: *(p.32)*
    a.   define the mission of the organization.
    b.   translate the firm's business mission into the goals and objectives of the organization.
    c.   analyze the current organizational structure and evaluate strategies and opportunities for growth that are consistent with its mission and objectives.
    d.   none of the above.

3. A mission statement usually covers the following basic areas: *(p.32)*
    a. the overall purpose of the organization.
    b. what the organization intends to achieve in terms of its customers and products.
    c. what the organization intends to achieve in terms of its resources.
    d. all of the above.

4. Individual units within the firm that operate like separate businesses, with each having its own mission, business objectives, resources, managers, and competitors are called: *(p.35)*
    a. corporate operating units (COUs).
    b. the firm's competencies.
    c. strategic business units (SBUs).
    d. the firm's benefits.

5. The Boston Consulting Group (BCG) matrix provides a portfolio management strategy in which: *(p.36)*
    a. existing, successful products generate cash that is used for investment in new products.
    b. a detailed assessment of the SBU is based on industry attractiveness and company business strengths.
    c. the grid allows a firm to place its strategic business units into nine different categories based on high, medium, and low industry attractiveness and business strengths.
    d. the process focuses on the firm's product mix and determines whether the firm would be better off putting its resources into existing products or trying to grow by developing or acquiring new products.

6. Cash cows are: *(p.37)*
    a. business units with low market shares in fast-growth markets.
    b. business units with a small share of a slow-growth market.
    c. business units having a dominant market share in a low-growth potential market.
    d. business units having a dominant market share in fast-growth markets.

7. Growth strategies that emphasize both new products and new markets are known as: *(p.38)*
    a. product development.
    b. diversification.
    c. market development.
    d. cost leadership.

8. _____ are business units with a dominant market share in high-growth markets. *(p.37)*
    a. Dogs.
    b. Question Marks.
    c. Cash Cows.
    d. Stars.

9. Properties of products that set them apart from competitors' products by providing unique customer benefits are called: *(p.41)*
    a. distinctive competencies.
    b. differential benefits.
    c. comparative advantages.
    d. consumer superiority.

10. The internal environment of an organization includes: *(p.34)*
    a. the uncontrollable elements outside of an organization that may effect its performance either positively or negatively.
    b. everything from consumers to government regulations to competitors to the overall economy.
    c. the controllable elements inside an organization including its people, its facilities, and how it does things that influence the operations of the organization.
    d. all of the above.

11. Once marketing management has identified the firm's strengths and weaknesses, and examined opportunities and threats in the external environment, the next step in the planning process is: *(p.35)*
    a. to develop objectives.
    b. to select a target market.
    c. to develop specific strategies.
    d. to prepare a marketing plan.

12. A product strategy: *(p.44)*
    a. includes pricing objectives and states the specific prices to be charged for a product.
    b. determines what design is best for the product, what features it will have, how it will be packaged, and what warranty it will carry.
    c. includes plans for advertising, consumer sales promotion, trade promotions, the sales function, publicity, and point-of purchase materials.
    d. describes how the product will be made available to targeted customers when and where they want it.

13. The implementation sections of a marketing plan contain: *(p.47)*
    a. a marketing budget.
    b. development of specific action plans.
    c. the assignment of major areas of responsibility to individuals or teams.
    d. all of the above.

14. Product development strategies: *(p.38)*
    a. create growth by selling new products in existing markets.
    b. introduce existing products to new markets.
    c. seek to increase sales of existing products to current customers, nonusers, and users of competing brands in served markets.
    d. emphasize both new products and new markets to achieve growth.

15. A functional structure separates marketing into: *(p.48)*
    a. customer needs or usage by geographic region.
    b. a product or brand.
    c. distinct components, such as advertising, sales promotion, sales force management and marketing research.
    d. sales and market share trends.

CHAPTER IN REVIEW—WRITING TO LEARN

1. Describe how a firm gains a competitive advantage.

    _____

    _____

    _____

    _____

2. Discuss the role of marketing strategies in the planning and the development of a marketing plan.

    _____

    _____

    _____

    _____

3. Explain the factors involved in the implementation and control of the marketing plan.

    _____

    _____

    _____

    _____

CASE ANALYSIS

Real People, Real Decisions: Meet Rahul Raj, Meal Exchange

Reread the three sections comprising the Meal Exchange vignette in Chapter 2 and answer the following questions:

1. What would be an appropriate mission statement for Meal Exchange if the company chose to pursue Option 1, described on page 43?

2. What type of planning—strategic, tactical or operational—is Rahul Raj currently engaged in? Why?

3. What are Meal Exchange's two main opportunities?

4. What is one of the main threats facing Meal Exchange?

SCENARIO

You are the Director of Marketing for a new National Basketball Association (NBA) team. While the team is not expected to make the playoffs for several years, you still have seats to fill for the coming season. The team's general manager and coach make most of the "product" decisions, with respect to who will be on the team, how often they will play and for how long. However, there are still many decisions left for you to make with respect to the target market and the marketing mix. You have a meeting next week with the team's general manager to discuss strategic planning.

Prepare answers to the following questions:

1. What are your major target markets?
2. Aside from the team itself, which other products might you consider offering for sale?
3. How will you approach pricing?
4. Propose four communication activities you would undertake to encourage customers to buy tickets.

ANSWERS

Chapter Outline

I.   STRATEGIC PLANNING: GUIDING THE BUSINESS
       Strategic Planning—A managerial decision process that matches an organization's resources and capabilities to its market opportunities for long-term growth and survival.
       Tactical Planning—A decision process that concentrates on developing detailed plans for strategies and tactics for the short term that support an organization's long-term strategic plan.
       Operational Planning—A decision process that focuses on developing detailed plans for day-to-day activities that carry out an organization's tactical plans.
       Cross-Functional Planning—An approach to tactical planning in which managers work together in developing tactical plans for each functional area in the firm, so that each plan considers the objectives of the other areas.

   A.   Defining the Organization's Business Mission—Top management's vision of why the firm exists and how it will differ from other firms and the place in the market it wants to take.
          Mission Statement—A formal statement in an organization's strategic plan that describes the overall purpose of the organization and what it intends to achieve in terms of its customers, products, and resources.

   B.   Evaluating the Environment: SWOT Analysis—An analysis of an organization's strengths and weaknesses and the opportunities and threats in its external environment.
          1.   Internal Environment—The controllable elements inside an organization including its people, its facilities, and how it does things that influence the operations of the organization.
          2.   External Environment—The uncontrollable elements outside of a organization that may affect its performance either positively or negatively.

   C.   Setting Organizational Objectives—In the next stage of the strategic planning process, top management translates the firm's business mission into specific goals called objectives.
          Objectives—Specific accomplishments, or outcomes that an organization hopes to achieve by a specific time.

   D.   Planning for Growth
          1.   Portfolio Analysis: Strategic Business Units
                 Strategic Business Units—Individual units within the firm that operate like separate businesses, with each having its own mission, business and marketing objectives, resources, managers, and competitors.
                 Business portfolio—The group of different businesses, products, or brands owned by an organization and characterized by different income-generating and growth capabilities.
                 Portfolio Analysis—A management tool for evaluating a firm's business mix and assessing the potential of an organization's strategic business units.
          2.   The Boston Consulting Group Matrix—Provides a portfolio management strategy in which existing, successful products generate cash that is used for investment in new products.
                       Stars—Get all the firm's attention and huge investments. Stars are business units with a dominant market share in high-growth markets.
                       Cash Cows—Business units having a dominant market share in a low-growth potential market.
                       Question Marks—Business units with low market shares in fast-growth markets.
                       Dogs—Business units with a small share of a slow-growth market.

3. Product-Market Growth Matrix—An assessment of the growth potential of existing markets and of entering new markets.

    Market Penetration—Growth strategies designed to increase sales of existing products to current customers, non-users, and users of competitive brands in served markets.

    Market Development—Growth strategies that introduce existing products to new markets.

    Product Development—Growth strategies that focus on selling new products in served markets.

    Diversification—Growth strategies that emphasize both new products and new markets.

II. THE MARKETING PLANNING PROCESS
    A. Creating a Competitive Advantage: Marketing's Strategic Focus

Competitive Advantage—The ability of a firm to outperform the competition, providing customers with a benefit the competition cannot.

        1. Identifying Distinctive Competencies

Distinctive Competency—A superior capability of a firm in comparison to its direct competitors.

        2. Providing Differential Benefits

Differential Benefits—Properties of products that set them apart from competitors' products by providing unique benefits.

    B. Setting Marketing Objectives
        1. Sales Objectives—One or more quantitative goals relating to sales.
        2. Product-Oriented Objectives—A growth strategy that focuses on product development.
        3. Market Objectives—Firms that determine that growth can be achieved with new customers using either market development strategies or diversification strategies.

III. DEVELOPING MARKETING STRATEGIES: ELEMENTS OF A MARKET PLAN
    A. Selecting a Target Market—A market segment the firm selects because it believes that its offerings are most suited to winning customers in that market.

    B. Developing Marketing Mix Programs—Identifying how marketing will accomplish its objectives in the firm's target markets.
        1. Product Strategies—Marketers decide which product(s) to market to each segment targeted and which characteristics of the product, e.g., design, packaging, branding, warranty, will provide the unique benefits targeted customers want.
        2. Pricing Strategies—A pricing strategy includes pricing objectives and states the specific prices to be charged for a product.
        3. Communication Strategies—Address issues such as which product message should be developed, how to deliver the message, and the mix of advertising, sales promotion, and personal selling that will be used.
        4. Distribution Strategies—Describes how the product will be made available to targeted customers when and where they want it.

    C. Preparing a Marketing Plan—A document that describes the marketing environment, outlines the marketing objectives, and identifies who will be responsible for carrying out each part of the marketing strategy.

Situation Analysis—The first part of a marketing plan that provides a thorough description of the firm's current situation including its internal and external environments.

IV. IMPLEMENTATION AND CONTROL OF THE MARKETING PLAN
  A. Implementing the Marketing Plan—The stage of the strategic management process in which strategies are put into action on a day-to-day basis.
    1. The Marketing Budget—A statement of the total amount to be spent on marketing and the allocation of money for each activity under a marketer's control.
    2. Organizing the Marketing Function—A functional structure separates marketing into distinct components, such as advertising, sales promotion, sales force management, and marketing research. A geographic structure is established when firms feel that customer needs differ by geographic region. A product structure may include a number of different brand managers and product group line managers, each of whom is responsible for an entire brand.

  B. Controlling the Marketing Plan—Measuring actual performance, comparing it to planned performance, and making necessary changes in plans and implementation.
    1. Trend Analysis—An analysis of past industry or company sales data to determine patterns of change that may continue into the future.
    2. Marketing Research—The methods used by a firm to obtain feedback on marketing activities.
    3. The Marketing Audit—A comprehensive review of a firm's marketing function.

Key Terms

1. Strategic planning
2. Operational planning
3. Mission statement
4. Objectives
5. Business portfolio
6. Portfolio analysis
7. Market penetration
8. Market development
9. Cross-functional planning
10. Competitive advantage
11. Distinctive competency
12. Marketing plan
13. Implementation
14. Marketing budget
15. Control

Multiple Choice

1. b
2. a
3. d
4. c
5. a
6. c
7. b
8. d
9. b
10. c
11. a
12. b
13. d
14. a
15. c

Chapter in Review—Writing to Learn

1. A competitive advantage means that a firm has developed reasons for customers to select its product over all others in the market. A firm gains a competitive advantage when it has distinctive competencies or capabilities that are stronger than those of the competition, and is able to provide differential or product benefits that are uniquely different from the competition. Creating a competitive advantage is the strategic focus of an organization's marketing planning process.

2.   The marketing planning process determines which strategies and action plans the firm will use to achieve its marketing objectives and its overall strategic goals. Marketing selects the target market(s) the organization will focus on, and determines which marketing mix strategies will be used to meet the needs of that market. Product strategies include decisions about products and product characteristics that will appeal to the target market. Pricing strategies state the specific prices to be charged and are influenced both by the cost of the marketing mix elements and targeted customers' willingness to pay. Communications strategies include plans for advertising and personal selling to reach the target market. Distribution strategies outline how the product will be made available to targeted customers when and where they want. The final step in the marketing planning process is the development of a written marketing plan that describes the firm's current situation, states the marketing objectives, identifies the specific strategies and action plans that will be used, and outlines how the plan will be implemented and controlled. It may include contingency plans that will be used if objectives are not met using initial strategies.

3.   Implementation or putting the plan into action includes development of the marketing budget, often using a percentage-of-sales or an objective-and-task method. Also essential to successful implementation is effective organization of the marketing function—that is, how the work is broken up into different jobs and assigned to different people. Control is the measurement of actual performance and comparison with planned performance. Planners may use trend analyses or other forms of marketing research to obtain performance feedback. A comprehensive review of the marketing system is sometimes conducted using a marketing audit.

Case Analysis

1.   A possible mission statement that reflects Option 1 would be: "Providing students worldwide with meal solutions".

2.   He is involved in strategic planning, because he is trying to answer fundamental questions such as: "What is our business about?" and "Which customers should we serve?"

3.   The main opportunities facing Meal Exchange are geographic expansion and the possibility of introducing new products into the marketplace.

4.   One of the main threats facing Meal Exchange is the possibility of competition entering the market.

CHAPTER 3

Decision Making in the New Era of Marketing: Enriching the Marketing Environment

CHAPTER OVERVIEW

In this chapter, we learned that firms in the New Era of Marketing emphasize social profit as well as economic profit. Companies behave ethically because it is morally right and because it allows them to earn goodwill, which helps them achieve economic goals.

Social responsibility means that New Era firms act in ways that benefit the public, the community, and the natural environment. New Era firms also practice social responsibility by promoting cultural diversity—that is, by actively seeking to include people of different sexes, ethnic groups, and religions as customers, suppliers, employees, and distribution channel members.

We considered how quality-focused firms in the New Era of marketing strive to provide goods and services that go beyond customer expectations with respect to the relationship between cost and value. Total quality management (TQM) is a management philosophy that focuses on satisfying the customer and reducing production costs through such programs as continuous quality improvement, employee empowerment, and a team approach that involves employees in all levels of the organization in cross-functional planning and task-related activities.

Next, we learned about the importance of an organization's internal environment. Success in the New Era of marketing rests heavily on an organization's corporate culture, the set of shared values, attitudes, beliefs that influence its decisions and practices. Another aspect of the internal environment in New Era firms is the value placed on the firm's relationship with its suppliers, intermediaries, competitors, and various publics.

Finally, we reviewed why marketers scan an organization's external business environment. Specifically, we considered how important it is to understand the economic, competitive, natural, technological, legal and sociocultural environments, and to integrate them into marketing planning.

CHAPTER OBJECTIVES

1. Explain why organizations have adopted a New Era marketing orientation focus on ethics and social responsibility.

2. Describe the New Era emphasis on quality.

3.   Discuss some of the important aspects of an organization's internal environment.

4.   Explain why marketers scan an organization's external business environment.

CHAPTER OUTLINE

With reference to the textbook, please provide a brief description of each of the main elements listed in the Chapter Outline below. The page numbers will help guide you through the learning process.

I.   WELCOME TO THE NEW ERA OF MARKETING _____ *(p.56)*
        Social Profit _____ *(p.56)*
        A.   Ethical Behaviour in the Marketplace
                Business Ethics _____ *(p.57)*
                1.   Code of Ethics _____ *(p.57)*
                2.   The High Costs of Unethical Marketplace
                        Behaviour _____ *(p.59)*
                3.   Consumerism: Fighting Back
                        Consumerism _____ *(p.60)*
                        CAC's Consumer Rights_____ *(p.60)*

        B.   Ethics in the Marketing _____ *(p.61)*
                1.   Making a Product Safe _____ *(p.61)*
                2.   Pricing the Product Fairly _____ *(p.61)*
                3.   Promoting the Product Ethically _____ *(p.61)*
                4.   Getting the Product Where It Belongs ___ *(p.62)*

        C.   Social Responsibility: Serving the Environment_____ *(p.62)*
                Environmental Stewardship_____ *(p.62)*
                1.   Green Marketing _____ *(p.64)*

        D.   Serving Society: Cause Marketing _____ *(p.65)*

        E.   Serving the Community: Promoting Cultural Diversity _____ *(p.65)*

II.   DOING IT WELL: A FOCUS ON QUALITY _____ *(p.66)*
        A.   Total Quality Management _____ *(p.66)*
                1.   ISO 9000 _____ *(p.66)*
                2.   Adding a Dose of Quality to the Marketing Mix ____ *(p.67)*

III.   THE INTERNAL BUSINESS ENVIRONMENT/CORPORATE RESOURCES AND
COMPETENCIES

    A.   Corporate Culture _____ *(p.69)*

        1.   Risk-Taking Cultures _____ *(p.69)*

        2.   Profit-Centred Versus People-Centred Cultures _____ *(p.69)*

    B.   Relationships with Publics_____ *(p.69)*

        Publics _____ *(p.69)*

        1.   Relationships with Suppliers and Intermediaries ____ *(p.69)*

        2.   Relationships with Competitors _____ *(p.70)*

        3.   Relationships with the Public _____ *(p.70)*

IV.   SCANNING THE EXTERNAL BUSINESS ENVIRONMENT ____ *(p.70)*

    A.   The Economic Environment _____ *(p.71)*

        1.   The Business Cycle: What Goes Around,

            Comes Around _____ *(p.71)*

        2.   The Power of Expectations _____ *(p.71)*

            Consumer Confidence_____ *(p.71)*

    B.   The Competitive Environment _____ *(p.72)*

        1.   Analyzing the Competition_____ *(p.72)*

            Competitive Intelligence _____ *(p.72)*

        2.   Competition in the Micro Environment

            Discretionary Income _____ *(p.72)*

            Product Competition _____ *(p.72)*

            Brand Competition _____ *(p.72)*

        3.   Competition in the Macro Environment

            Monopoly _____ *(p.73)*

            Perfect Competition _____ *(p.73)*

            Oligopoly _____ *(p.73)*

            Monopolistic Competition _____ *(p.73)*

    C.   The Technological Environment_____ *(p.73)*

        1.   Patent_____ *(p.74)*

    D.   The Legal Environment_____ *(p.74)*

        1.   The Watchdogs of Business: Regulatory Agencies __ *(p.75)*

        2.   Adapting to a Regulatory Environment _____ *(p.75)*

    E.   The Sociocultural Environment_____ *(p.76)*

        1.   Demographics _____ *(p.76)*

KEY TERMS

Select the correct term for each definition and write it in the space provided.

Social responsibility
Corporate culture
Business cycle
Cause marketing
Social profit
Monopoly
Cultural diversity
Business ethics

Total quality management (TQM)
Consumer confidence
Demographics
Consumerism
Quality
Patent
Seven Consumer Rights

1. _Social profit_

   The benefit an organization and society receive from its ethical practices, community service, efforts to promote cultural diversity, and concern for the natural environment. *(p.56)*

2. _Business ethics_

   Rules of conduct for an organization that are standards against which most people in its environment judge what is right and what is wrong. *(p.57)*

3. _Consumerism_

   A social movement directed toward protecting consumers from harmful business practices. *(p.60)*

4. _Seven Consumer Rights_

   Rights that the Consumers' Association of Canada agrees both government and ethical businesses should recognize and provide. *(p.61)*

5. _Social responsibility_

   A management practice in which organizations seek to engage in activities that have a positive effect on society and promote the public good. *(p.62)*

6. _Cause marketing_

   A marketing strategy in which an organization seeks to serve its community by promoting and supporting a worthy cause or by allying itself with non-profit organizations to tackle a social problem. *(p.65)*

7. _Culture diversity_

A management practice that actively seeks to include people of different sexes, races, ethnic groups, and religions in an organization's employees, customers, suppliers, and distribution channel partners. *(p.65)*

8. _Quality_

The level of performance, reliability, features, safety, cost and other product characteristics that consumers expect to satisfy their needs and wants. *(p.66)*

9. _TQM_
Total quality management

A management philosophy that focuses on satisfying customers though empowering employees to be an active part of continuous quality improvement. *(p.66)*

10. _Corporate culture_

The set of values, norms, beliefs, and practices held by an organization's managers, and that influence the behaviour of everyone in the organization. *(p.69)*

11. _patent_

Legal document granting an individual or firm exclusive right to produce and sell a particular invention. *(p.74)*

12. _Business cycle_

The overall patterns of change in the economy including periods of prosperity, recession, depression, and recovery, which affect consumer and business purchasing power. *(p.71)*

13. _Consumer confidence_

An indicator of future spending patterns as measured by the extent to which people are optimistic or pessimistic about the state of the economy. *(p.71)*

14. _monopoly_

A market situation in which one firm, the only supplier of a particular product, is able to control the price, quality, and supply of that product. *(p.73)*

15. _Demographics_

Statistics that measure observable aspects of a population, including age, gender, ethnic group, income, education, occupation, and family structure. *(p.76)*

MULTIPLE CHOICE

Identify the most correct answer.

1. Business ethics is where: *(p.56)*
   a. the firm takes its first step toward creating social profit.
   b. consumer interests are least important.
   c. the marketers' interests are in the forefront.
   d. all of the above.

2. When a consumer purchases an item of clothing such as a party dress or an expensive business suit, wears it for a special occasion, and returns it the next day as if it had not been worn, this is called: *(p.60)*
   a. consumer sovereignty.
   b. rebate scamming.
   c. caveat emptor syndrome.
   d. retailing borrowing.

3. A pricing strategy that is unethical but not illegal is: *(p.61)*
   a. price discrimination strategy.
   b. price gouging.
   c. price-fixing.
   d. none of the above.

4. Slotting allowances are: *(p.63)*
   a. fees paid by casinos in Las Vegas for marketing slot machines.
   b. lower prices charged by a manufacturer to larger customers.
   c. fees many large retailers are forcing manufacturers to pay for agreeing to stock the company's products on valuable shelf space.
   d. price increases of popular products.

5. Environmental stewardship is: *(p.62)*
   a. a management practice in which organizations seek to engage in activities that have a positive effect on society and promote the public good.
   b. a position taken by an organization to protect or enhance the natural environment as it conducts its business activities.
   c. a social movement directed towards protecting consumers from harmful environmental factors.
   d. supporting the Environmental Bill of Rights.

6. A marketing strategy that supports environmental stewardship by creating an environmentally-founded differential benefit in the minds of consumers is called: *(p.62)*
   a. green marketing.
   b. cause marketing.
   c. environmental diversity.
   d. social responsibility.

7. Social profit is: *(p.56)*
   a. a firm's success in achieving dollar profit.
   b. the income statement that shows the economic bottom line of a firm.
   c. the net benefit both the firm and society receive from a firm's ethical practices and socially responsible behaviour.
   d. how the firm's profit impacts society.

8. We call efforts to do business *right* and do it *well*: *(p.56)*
   a. the Product Era of marketing.
   b. the Social Era of marketing.
   c. the Public Era of marketing.
   d. the New Era of marketing.

9. A philosophy that calls for company-wide dedication to the development, maintenance, and continuous improvement of all aspects of the company's operations is called: *(p.66)*
   a. Kaizen.
   b. TQM.
   c. participatory management program.
   d. relationship marketing.

10. The International Standards Organization: *(p.66)*
    a. is an organization that initially developed a set of criteria in 1987 to regulate product quality in Canada.
    b. is an organization that tests and approves the design and manufacturing processes to assure the safety of the products.
    c. developed a broad set of guidelines, known as ISO 9000, to cover issues related to the manufacture and installation of products, as well as post-sale servicing.
    d. all of the above.

11. Groups of people—including suppliers, channel intermediaries, customers, employees, shareholders, financial institutions, government, the media, and public interest groups—that have interest in an organization are called: *(p.69)*
    a. publics.
    b. business partners.
    c. intermediaries.
    d. activists.

12. The Business Cycle: *(p.71)*
    a. is both a measure of the current state of the economy and a predictor of future economic trends.
    b. represents the total value of goods and services produced in a country, regardless of whether the firms are Canadian or foreign-owned.
    c. grows at about 3 percent per year in Canada.
    d. includes periods of prosperity, recovery, recession, and depression.

13. A marketing situation in which competitors offering very different products compete to satisfy the same consumer needs and wants is known as: *(p.72)*
    a. brand competition.
    b. product competition.
    c. discretionary competition.
    d. consumer competition.

14. A market structure in which a relatively small number of sellers, each holding a substantial share of the market, compete in a market with many buyers is called: *(p.73)*
    a. perfect competition.
    b. monopolistic competition.
    c. oligopoly.
    d. adversarial competition.

15. The portion of income people have left after paying for such necessities as housing, utilities, food and clothing is called: *(p.72)*
    a. discretionary income.
    b. diversionary income.
    c. gross income.
    d. net income.

CHAPTER IN REVIEW—WRITING TO LEARN

1. Explain why New Era organizations focus on ethics and social responsibility.

    _____

    _____

    _____

    _____

2. Describe the New Era emphasis on quality.

    _____

    _____

    _____

    _____

3.   Discuss some of the important aspects of an organization's internal environment.

_____

_____

_____

_____

CASE ANALYSIS

Real People, Real Decisions: Meet Margaret Yee, Ethical Funds

Reread the three sections comprising the Ethical Funds vignette in Chapter 3 and answer the following questions:

1.   Which two *external* environmental factors have led to increased demand for mutual funds, RRSPs and RESPs?

2.   What is Ethical Funds' main source of competitive advantage in the mutual fund market?

3.   Which aspects of the *internal* environment at Ethical Funds have supported efforts to build strong brand performance?

4.   Which "publics" is Margaret Yee particularly concerned with as she weighs her options?

SCENARIO

You are the inventor of a new technology. The technology prevents cell phones from ringing in places like restaurants, movie theatres, classrooms or anywhere else the purchaser of this "jamming" technology might wish to use it. The purchaser installs the device in the chosen location, preventing patrons in that physical space from receiving incoming calls. Because the device blocks all calls, it will also prevent calls from reaching cell phones that vibrate when a call is received. However, all patrons will still be able to make outgoing calls.

You believe your product will be an enormous success—many people are upset with rude restaurant patrons who receive calls in the middle of dinner—not to mention the many professors who find themselves stopping in mid-sentence at the sound of a ringing phone.

There is a lot to look into before launching the product. You decide to begin by scanning your external environment, looking for answers to the following questions:

1. Who is your competition—and where can you find out information about them?
2. Can you patent your invention? Visit the Canadian Intellectual Property Office at http://cipo.gc.ca to see whether a similar device has already received a patent in Canada.
3. Which sociocultural trends might affect the adoption of your invention?
4. Which legal and regulatory issues should concern you?

ANSWERS

Chapter Outline

I. WELCOME TO THE NEW ERA OF MARKETING
    New Era marketers have come to realize that decisions and strategies designed to satisfy consumer needs and wants must not only be economically sound—they must also have a strong ethical foundation and be socially responsible as well.
    Social Profit—The benefit an organization and society receive from its ethical practices, community service, efforts to promote cultural diversity, and concern for the natural environment.

    A. Ethical Behaviour in the Marketplace
        Business Ethics—Rules of conduct for an organization that are standards against which most people in its environments judge what is right and what is wrong.

        1. Code of Ethics—Written standards of behaviour to which everyone in the organization must subscribe.
        2. The High Costs of Unethical Marketplace Behaviour—In the New Era of marketing, managers understand that ethical behaviour is not only the right way to act, it also serves the best interests of the organization.
        3. Consumerism: Fighting Back
            Consumerism—A social movement directed toward protecting consumers from harmful business practices.
            Consumers' Association of Canada's Seven Consumer Rights—The rights of consumers to safety, to be informed, to be heard, to redress, to choose, to a healthy environment and to consumer education.

    B. The Role of Ethics in the Marketing Mix—New Era Managers also take into account the ethical side of each of the 4 P's in the marketing mix.

        1. Making a Product Safe—In developing product strategies, marketing management's key ethical decisions relate to product safety.
        2. Pricing the Product Fairly—Many pricing practices are now illegal (price-fixing, and price discrimination).
        3. Promoting the Product Ethically—To protect consumers from being misled, the Canadian Code of Advertising Standards has specific guidelines regarding unfair or deceptive advertising.
        4. Getting the Product Where It Belongs—The way a firm chooses to get its products to the place where consumers want them, at the time they want them, can also involve ethical decisions.

    C. Social Responsibility: Serving the Environment—A management practice in which organizations seek to engage in activities that have a positive effect on society and promote the public good.
        Environmental Stewardship—A position taken by an organization to protect or enhance the natural environment as it conducts its business activities.

        1. Green Marketing—A marketing strategy that supports environmental stewardship by creating an environmentally founded differential benefit in the minds of consumers.

    D. Serving Society: Cause Marketing—A marketing strategy in which an organization seeks to serve its community by promoting and supporting a worthy cause or by allying itself with non-profit organizations to tackle a social problem.

    E. Serving the Community: Promoting Cultural Diversity—A management practice that actively seeks to include people of different sexes, races, ethnic groups, and religions in an organization's employees, customers, suppliers, and distribution channel partners.

II.   DOING IT WELL: A FOCUS ON QUALITY—The level of performance, reliability, features, safety and other product characteristics that consumers expect to satisfy their needs and wants.
    A.   Total Quality Management—A management philosophy that focuses on satisfying customers through empowering employees to be an active part of continuous quality improvement.
        1.   ISO 9000—Criteria developed by the International Standards Organization to regulate product quality.
        2.   Adding a Dose of Quality to the Marketing Mix—New Era firms continually seek ways to improve product, place, price, and promotion.

III. THE INTERNAL BUSINESS ENVIRONMENT/CORPORATE RESOURCES AND COMPETENCIES
    A.   Corporate Culture—The set of values, norms, beliefs that influence the behaviour of everyone in the organization.
        1.   Risk-Taking Cultures—Firms that value innovativeness, individuality, and creativity.
        2.   Profit-Centred Versus People-Centred Cultures—In New Era firms, where the business mission includes a concern for employees, customers, and society, as well as shareholder profits.

    B.   Relationships With Publics—A measure of a firm's internal strengths relates to the relationships it develops outside the organization.
       Publics—Groups of people—including suppliers, channel intermediaries, customers, employees, shareholders, financial institutions, government, the media and public interest groups—that have an interest in an organization.
        1.   Relationships with Suppliers and Intermediaries—New Era firms know that they can't make quality products if they can't get quality parts from their suppliers.
        2.   Relationships with Competitors—Firms often find it is to their advantage to cooperate with others in the same business.
        3.   Relationships with the Public—Companies need to be sensitive to the concerns of various citizens' groups.

IV.   SCANNING THE EXTERNAL BUSINESS ENVIRONMENT—Firms scan the external business environment and respond to trends in a way that results in both economic and social profit.
    A.   The Economic Environment—This means evaluating factors that influence consumer and business buying patterns.
        1.   The Business Cycle: What Goes Around, Comes Around—The overall patterns of change in the economy—including periods of prosperity, recession, depression, and recovery—that affect consumer and business purchasing power.
        2.   The Power of Expectations—Many economists suggest that changes in the economy are primarily a "self-fulfilling prophecy."
        Consumer Confidence—An indicator of future spending patterns as measured by the extent to which people are optimistic or pessimistic about the state of the economy.

    B.   The Competitive Environment—Successful firms take the lead and keep ahead of the competition.
        1.   Analyzing the Competition—Before a firm can begin to develop strategies that will create a competitive advantage in the marketplace, it has to know who its competitors are and what they're doing.
        Competitive Intelligence—The process of gathering and analyzing public information about rival firms.
        2.   Competition in the Micro Environment
        Discretionary Income—The portion of income people have left over after paying for necessities such as housing, utilities, food, and clothing.
        Product Competition—-When firms offering different products compete to satisfy the same consumer needs and wants.
        Brand Competition—A marketing situation in which firms offering similar products or services, compete for consumers based on their brand's reputation or perceived benefits.

3.   Competition in the Macro Environment

Monopoly—A market situation in which one firm, the only supplier of a particular product, is able to control the price, quality, and supply of that product.

Oligopoly—A market structure in which a relatively small number of sellers, each holding a substantial share of the market, compete in a market with many buyers.

Monopolistic Competition—A market structure in which many firms, each having slightly different products, offer consumers unique benefits.

Perfect Competition—A market structure in which many small sellers, all of whom offer similar products, are unable to have an impact on the quality, price, or supply of a product.

C.   The Technological Environment—Technological developments that impact marketers today include the improved abilities of organizations to communicate with customers, complete transactions more effectively, and deliver goods and services more efficiently.

1.   Patent—Legal document granting an individual or firm exclusive right to produce and sell a particular invention.

D.   The Legal Environment—Include all laws that affect businesses

1.   The Watchdogs of Business: Regulatory Agencies—Federal and provincial governments have also created a host of regulatory agencies, to monitor business activities and enforce laws.

2.   Adapting to a Regulatory Environment—New Era firms know that the best of all worlds is when no government regulation is needed because firms work together to make sure everyone plays fair.

E.   The Sociocultural Environment—In both consumer and business-to-business markets, an understanding of social and cultural factors is a must.

1.   Demographics—Statistics that measure observable aspects of a population, including age, gender ethnic group, income, education, occupation, and family structure.

Key Terms   *Multiple Choice*

	Key Terms		Multiple Choice
1.	Social profit	1.	a
2.	Business ethics	2.	d
3.	Consumerism	3.	b
4.	Seven Consumer Rights	4.	c
5.	Social responsibility	5.	b
6.	Cause marketing	6.	a
7.	Cultural diversity	7.	c
8.	Quality	8.	d
9.	Total quality management (TQM)	9.	b
10.	Corporate culture	10.	c
11.	Patent	11.	a
12.	Business cycle	12.	d
13.	Consumer confidence	13.	b
14.	Monopoly	14.	c
15.	Demographics	15.	a

Chapter in Review — Writing to Learn

1. Firms in the New Era of Marketing emphasize social profit as well as economic profit. Companies behave ethically because it is morally right and because it allows them to earn goodwill that helps them achieve economic goals. New Era marketers consider ethical issues in developing marketing strategies and are often influenced by consumerism, a social movement aimed at protecting consumers from harmful business practices.

    Social responsibility means that New Era firms act in ways that benefit the public, the community, and the natural environment. New Era marketers assume social responsibility through environmental stewardship, in which the firm's actions either improve or do not harm the natural environment, and cause marketing, which focus on market strategies that promote the public good.

2. Quality-focused firms in the New Era of marketing strive to provide goods and services that go beyond customer expectations about the relationship between cost and value. Total quality management (TQM) is a management philosophy that focuses on satisfying customers and reducing production costs through such programs a continuous quality improvement, employee empowerment, and a team approach that involves employees in all levels of the organization in cross-functional planning and task-related activities.

3. Success in the New Era of marketing rests heavily on an organization's corporate culture, the set of shared values, attitudes, beliefs that influence its decisions and practices. New Era firms are more people-centred and concerned with the welfare of employees. Another aspect of the internal environment in New Era firms is the value placed on the firm's relationships with its suppliers, intermediaries, competitors, and various publics. Important publics include employees, shareholders, government, media, financial institutions, and consumers.

Case Analysis

1. The two environmental factors that have led to increased demand for these products are low interest rates and government tax incentives.

2. A survey found that 98% of Canadians surveyed prefer to invest in socially responsible companies—this is the main source of Ethical Funds' competitive advantage, as their funds meet this need, whereas many competitors' funds do not.

3. Educated employees and well-entrenched channels of distribution are two aspects of the internal environment that can support Ethical Funds' efforts to build strong brand performance.

4. As she weighs her options, Margaret Yee's main concern is with the potential reaction of her two main "publics": consumers and her distribution channel, the credit unions.

CHAPTER 4

Think Globally and Act Locally: Marketing in a Multinational Environment

CHAPTER OVERVIEW

In this chapter, we discuss how global marketing opportunities can present a challenging and vast new frontier. We have discovered that firms choose to enter foreign markets for several reasons. However, the global game is not always easy to play. Competition comes from both local and foreign firms, and differences in national laws, customs, and consumer preferences can make it difficult for any business to achieve success.

A country's stage of economic development determines a global firm's marketing opportunities. In less developed countries with subsistence economies, opportunities are usually limited to staples and inexpensive discretionary items. In developing countries, such as those in Eastern Europe, Latin America, and the Pacific Rim, an industrial-based economy is evolving and the rising middle class creates great demand for basic consumer goods. Developed countries such as Japan have highly sophisticated marketing systems and offer almost limitless marketing opportunities for goods and services.

We then discussed how elements of the political, legal, and cultural environments influence a firm's decision to enter global markets. Finally, we considered the different strategies a firm can choose in order to enter global markets. Specifically, we discussed exporting, licensing, franchising, partnerships or strategic alliances, and mergers. Sometimes a firm might also evaluate the arguments for standardization versus localization of marketing strategies.

CHAPTER OBJECTIVES

1. Explain how complex relationships among firms, countries, and regions influence world trade.

2. Understand how political, legal, and cultural issues influence global marketing strategies and outcomes.

3. Explain the strategies a firm can use to enter global markets.

4. Understand the arguments for standardization versus localization of marketing strategies in global markets, and understand how elements of the marketing mix apply in international markets.

CHAPTER OUTLINE

With reference to the textbook, please provide a brief description of each of the main elements listed in the Chapter Outline below. The page numbers will help guide you through the learning process.

I.   LET'S GET SMALL _____ *(p.86)*
    A.   World Trade_____ *(p.88)*
        1.   How "Worldly" Can A Company Be?
            Domestic Firm_____ *(p.88)*
            Exporting Firm _____ *(p.89)*
            Multinational Firm _____ *(p.89)*
            Global Firm_____ *(p.89)*
        2.   Countertrade _____ *(p.89)*
        3.   Trade Flow _____ *(p.89)*

    B.   Competitive Advantage_____ *(p.90)*
        1.   Demand Conditions_____ *(p.90)*
        2.   Related and Supporting Industries _____ *(p.90)*
        3.   Factor Conditions _____ *(p.90)*
        4.   Company Strategy, Structure, and Rivalry _____ *(p.90)*

    C.   Borders, Roadblocks, and Communities
        1.   Protected Trade
            Protectionism_____ *(p.90)*
            Import Quotas _____ *(p.91)*
            Embargo _____ *(p.91)*
            Tariffs _____ *(p.91)*
            General Agreement on Tariffs and Trade (GATT) ___ *(p.91)*
            World Trade Organization (WTO) _____ *(p.91)*
         2.   Economic Communities _____ *(p.91)*
            North American Free Trade Agreement (NAFTA)___ *(p.91)*
            European Union (EU) _____ *(p.92)*

II.   THE GLOBAL MARKETING ENVIRONMENT_____ *(p.92)*
    A.   The Economic Environment _____ *(p.92)*
        1.   Indicators of Economic Health
            Standard of Living_____ *(p.92)*
            Gross Domestic Product _____ *(p.93)*
            Economic Infrastructure _____ *(p.93)*
         2.   Level of Economic Development
            Less Developed Country_____ *(p.93)*
            Developing Countries _____ *(p.93)*
            Developed Country _____ *(p.94)*

B.   The Political and Legal Environment _____ (p.94)
    1.   Political Issues
        Economic Sanctions _____ (p.94)
        Nationalization _____ (p.94)
        Expropriation_____ (p.95)
    2.   Regulatory Issues
        Local Content Rules _____ (p.95)
    3.   Human Rights Issues_____ (p.96)

C.   The Cultural Environment_____ (p.96)
    1.   Values
        Cultural Values _____ (p.96)
        Collectivist Culture _____ (p.96)
        Individualist Culture _____ (p.97)
    2.   Norms and Customs
        Norms _____ (p.97)
        Custom _____ (p.97)
        More _____ (p.97)
        Conventions _____ (p.98)
    3.   Symbols and Superstitions
        Semiotics_____ (p.99)
    4.   Language_____ (p.99)
    5.   Ethnocentricity
        Ethnocentrism _____ (p.100)

III.   HOW "GLOBAL" SHOULD A MARKETING STRATEGY BE?__ (p.101)
    A.   Company-Level Decisions: Choosing a
    Market Entry Strategy _____ (p.102)
        1.   Exporting
            Export Merchant _____ (p.102)
        2.   Contractual Agreements
            Licensing_____ (p.103)
            Franchising _____ (p.103)
        3.   Strategic Alliance _____ (p.103)
            Joint Venture_____ (p.103)
        4.   Direct Investment _____ (p.103)

    B.   Product-Level Decisions: Choosing a Marketing Mix
    Strategy _____ (p.104)
        1.   Standardization versus Localization _____ (p.104)
        2.   Product Decisions _____ (p.105)
        3.   Promotion Decisions_____ (p.107)
        4.   Price Decisions _____ (p.107)
            Grey Market _____ (p.108)
            Dumping _____ (p.108)
        5.   Distribution Decisions_____ (p.108)

KEY TERMS

Select the correct term for each definition and write it in the space provided.

Protectionism

Economic communities

Standardization

Trade flow

Franchising

General Agreement of Tariffs & Trade (GATT)

Demand conditions

Strategic alliance

Developing country

Joint venture

Export merchants

Nationalization

Licensing

Competitive advantage

Political risk assessment

1. _____ The pattern of economic interdependence among countries or regions. *(p.89)*

2. _____ The ability of a firm to outperform the competition, thereby providing customers with a benefit the competition can't. *(p.90)*

3. _____ A market condition in which a country's or market's population growth rate, economic condition, and other characteristics create high levels of demand and potential opportunities for businesses. *(p.90)*

4. _____ A country in which the economy is shifting from agriculture to industry. *(p.93)*

5. _____ Groups of countries that band together to promote trade among themselves and to make it easier for member nations to compete elsewhere. *(p.91)*

6. _____ A process in which international marketers weigh a foreign country's market potential against political conditions that may hinder market success. *(p.94)*

7. _____ A domestic government's seizure of a foreign company's assets without any compensation. *(p.95)*

8. _____ A government policy that gives domestic companies an advantage. *(p.90)*

9. _____ An international treaty to reduce import tax levels and trade restrictions. *(p.91)*

10. _____ An intermediary that a firm uses to represent it in another country. *(p.102)*

11. _____ An agreement in which one firm gives another firm the right to produce and market its product in a specified location in return for royalties. *(p.103)*

12. _____ A form of licensing involving the right to adapt an entire system of doing business. *(p.103)*

13. _____ The relationship developed between a firm seeking a deeper commitment to a foreign market and a domestic firm in the target country. *(p.103)*

14. _____ A strategic alliance in which two or more firms form a new entity, allowing the partners to pool their resources for common goals. *(p.103)*

15. _____ An international marketing perspective in which the same marketing mix strategies are used in all global markets. *(p.104)*

MULTIPLE CHOICE

Identify the most correct answer.

1. A country at the earliest stage of economic development is categorized as a: *(p.93)*
   a. less developed country (LDC).
   b. subsistence-economy country (SEC).
   c. limited-market country (LMC).
   d. technology-deficient country (TDC).

2. A developed country is characterized by: *(p.94)*
   a. weak private enterprise.
   b. strong private enterprise.
   c. market potential for limited goods and services.
   d. all of the above.

3. Government actions that prohibit or restrict trade with a particular country for political reasons are: *(p.94)*
   a. strategic alliances.
   b. closed trade zoning.
   c. global prohibition.
   d. economic sanctions.

4. Expropriation is: *(p.95)*
   a. a domestic government's seizure of a foreign company's assets without any compensation.
   b. voluntary payments by a foreign owner to get an illegal advantage.
   c. the official seizure of foreign-owned property in a country, frequently without full-value payment to the foreign owners.
   d. payment extracted under duress by someone in authority from a person seeking what they are lawfully entitled to.

5. A government trade regulation limiting the quantity of certain goods is allowed entry into a country is a(n): *(p.91)*
   a. tariff.
   b. quota.
   c. embargo.
   d. dumping.

6. A government trade regulation which prohibits specified foreign goods completely is called a(n): *(p. 91)*
   a. tariff.
   b. keiretsu.
   c. embargo.
   d. import quota.

7. A form of protectionism stipulating that a certain proportion of a product must consist of components supplied by industries in the host country is called: *(p.95)*
   a. domestic component law.
   b. the General Agreement of Tariffs and Trade.
   c. the Generalized System of Preferences.
   d. local content rule.

8. An exporting strategy: *(p.102)*
   a. allows a firm to sell its products in global markets.
   b. cushions the firm against downturns in its domestic market.
   c. allows the firm to maintain control over design and production decisions.
   d. all of the above.

9. A form of licensing involving the right to adapt an entire system of doing business. *(p.103)*
    a. franchising.
    b. subcontracting.
    c. outsourcing.
    d. joint venturing.

10. Ethnocentrism: *(p.100)*
    a. involves cooperation between two firms who work together on the same task.
    b. is the tendency to prefer products or people of one's own culture.
    c. is an agreement between firms that requires cooperation to market a new product.
    d. is also known as outsourcing.

11. A relationship between firms that requires a deeper commitment to a foreign market and a domestic firm in the target country is a: *(p.103)*
    a. strategic alliance.
    b. bilateral financial venture.
    c. financial investment alliance.
    d. strategic horizontal synergy.

12. Guideline(s) for choosing a standardized strategy over a localized strategy include: *(p.105)*
    a. low cost of R&D.
    b. unique cultural factors influencing consumption.
    c. high promotion via universal image.
    d. all of the above.

13. A firm encounters grey marketing practices in which of the following situations? *(p.108)*
    a. competing firms agree to coordinate pricing strategies.
    b. other foreign firms in a country deliberately undercut their prices to gain a foothold in the market.
    c. a company tries to get a toehold in a foreign market by pricing its products lower than they are offered at home.
    d. developing countries are allowed to export goods duty-free.

14. A custom with a strong moral overtone. *(p.97)*
    a. culture.
    b. conventions.
    c. norms.
    d. more.

15. An international marketing perspective in which marketing mix strategies are adapted for different global markets is called: *(p.105)*
    a. localization.
    b. comparative advantage.
    c. standardization.
    d. global market adaptation.

CHAPTER IN REVIEW—WRITING TO LEARN

1.   Explain why firms decide to seek global marketing opportunities.

_____

_____

_____

_____

2.   Describe how less developed, developing, and developed countries provide different global marketing opportunities.

_____

_____

_____

_____

3.   Discuss the arguments for standardization versus localization of marketing strategies.

_____

_____

_____

_____

CASE ANALYSIS

Real People, Real Decisions: Meet Peter Einstein, MTV Europe

Reread the three sections comprising the MTV Europe vignette in Chapter 4 and answer the following questions:

1. What were MTV's marketing objectives when it first entered the European market?

2. Would you classify MTV's initial approach to the European market as "standardization" or "localization"? Why?

3. Like many companies breaking into foreign markets, MTV faced a particular barrier. What was this barrier?

4. Which marketing mix elements did MTV adapt to "localize" its marketing strategy?

SCENARIO

You are a successful entrepreneur in Canada, where you and your partner have been producing and marketing low-cost lamps for over twenty years. Growth in your business has slowed considerably over the past five years, despite it being a time of general prosperity in the Canadian economy. You are beginning to wonder if there might be better opportunities elsewhere to grow your business. Because you speak both English and Spanish, and frequently vacation in Mexico, you decided to explore the opportunity of exporting your lamps on your next visit there.

You arrange a meeting with the President of a company that imports lamps and lighting fixtures from all over the world, and sells them to wholesalers and retailers throughout Mexico, Central America and South America. You discuss how your firms might collaborate, and the President suggests that you get back to him with a concrete proposal, after you have had an opportunity to consult with your partner.

You return to Canada the following week, and raise the issue with your business partner at your weekly meeting. Your partner raises the following questions, which you agree to research over the coming week:

1. Are there any import quotas, embargos or agreements that could restrict or enhance trade with Mexico? What are they and what is their impact?
2. What is the current state of the Mexican economy, and what is the country's level of economic development? Would lamps be a big seller there?
3. What type of contractual agreement, e.g., licensing, franchising, a strategic alliance or a joint venture, will you recommend and why?
4. Should the company opt for a standardization or localization strategy? Why?

ANSWERS

Chapter Outline

I.   LET'S GET SMALL—The world is becoming a smaller place, so the smart marketer needs to think globally by setting its sights on diverse markets around the world, but act locally by being willing to adapt its business practices to conditions in other parts of the globe.

    A.   World Trade—Many successful firms know that going global is an option they can't ignore.

        1.   How "Worldly" Can A Company Be?

        Domestic firm—Confines its sales and marketing efforts to its home market.

        Exporting firm—Expands sales by offering its products for sale in other countries.

        Multinational firm—Operates in many foreign markets, and modifies the product it sells accordingly.

        Global firm—Views the world as its market, and tends to operate the same way in many countries, adapting strategy when necessary to conform to local conditions.

        2.   Countertrade—Type of trade in which goods are paid for with other items instead of with cash.

        3.   Trade Flow—The pattern of economic interdependence among countries or regions.

    B.   Competitive Advantage—A company's success in both domestic and foreign markets depends on conditions in its home country that make it easier or harder to compete.

        1.   Demand Conditions—The number and sophistication of domestic customers for a product.

        2.   Related and Supporting Industries—Companies must have access to other firms that provide high-quality products and services they require to turn out competitive products.

        3.   Factor Conditions—The quality of a country's resources, including its infrastructure, the educational level of its people, and the availability of raw materials.

        4.   Company Strategy, Structure, and Rivalry—The way a country's businesses are organized and managed, and the intensity of competition that creates pressure to innovate.

    A.   Borders, Roadblocks, and Communities

        1.   Protected Trade

        Protectionism—Policy adopted by a government to give domestic companies an advantage.

        Import Quotas—Limitations set by a government on the amount of a product allowed to enter or leave a country.

        Embargo—A quota completely prohibiting specified goods from entering or leaving a country.

        Tariffs—Taxes on imported goods.

        General Agreement on Tariffs and Trade (GATT)— International Treaty to reduce import tax levels and trade restrictions.

        World Trade Organization (WTO)—Formed to mediate trade disputes between nations and to deal with cases in which unfair protectionism by one country is claimed by another.

        Economic Communities—Groups of countries that band together to promote trade among themselves and to make it easier for member nations to compete elsewhere.

        North American Free Trade Agreement (NAFTA)—The world's largest economic community composed of the United States, Canada, and Mexico.

        European Union (EU)—Economic community that now includes most of Western Europe.

II.   THE GLOBAL MARKETING ENVIRONMENT—How economic, political, and cultural factors affect marketers' global strategies.
  A.   The Economic Environment—Countries vary in terms of their economic development.
         1.   Indicators of Economic Health
                Standard of Living—An indicator of the average quality and quantity of goods and services consumed in a country.
                Gross Domestic Product—The total dollar value of goods and services produced by a nation in a year.
                Economic Infrastructure—The quality of a country's distribution, financial, and communications systems.
         2.   Level of Economic Development
                Less Developed Country—A country at the earliest stage of economic development.
                Developing Countries—Countries in which the economy is shifting its emphasis from agriculture to industry.
                Developed Country—A country that boasts sophisticated marketing systems, strong private enterprise, and bountiful market potential for many goods and services.

  B.   The Political and Legal Environment—When entering a foreign market, a firm must carefully weigh political and legal risks.
         1.   Political Issues
                Economic Sanctions—Trade prohibitions imposed by one country against another.
                Nationalization—A domestic government's takeover of a foreign company for its assets, with some reimbursement, though often not for the full value.
                Expropriation—A domestic government's seizure of a foreign company's assets without any compensation.
         2.   Regulatory Issues
                Local Content Rules—A form of protectionism stipulating that a certain proportion of a product must consist of components supplied by industries in the host country.
         3.   Human Rights Issues—Some governments and individual companies are especially vigilant about denying business opportunities to countries that mistreat their citizens.

  C.   The Cultural Environment—A firm needs to understand and adapt to the customs, characteristics, and practices of its citizens.
         1.   Values
                Cultural Values—A society's deeply held beliefs about right and wrong ways to live.
                Collectivist Culture—Culture in which people subordinate their personal goals to those of a stable community.
                Individualist Culture—Culture in which people tend to attach more importance to personal goals than to those of the larger community.
         2.   Norms and Customs
                Norms—Specific rules dictating what is right or wrong, acceptable or unacceptable.
                Custom—A norm handed down from the past that controls basic behaviours.
                More—A custom with a strong moral overtone.
                Conventions—Norms regarding the conduct of everyday life.
         3.   Symbols and Superstitions
                Semiotics—Field of study that examines how meanings are assigned to symbols.
         4.   Language—Language barriers can be big obstacles to marketers breaking into foreign markets.
         5.   Ethnocentricity
                Ethnocentrism—The tendency to prefer products or people of one's own culture.

III.   HOW "GLOBAL" SHOULD A GLOBAL MARKETING STRATEGY BE?—A company must decide on the nature of its commitment, including whether it will partner with another firm or go it alone.

A.   Company Level Decisions—A firm deciding to go global must determine the level of commitment it is willing to make to operate in another country.

1.   Exporting

Export Merchant—An intermediary used by a firm to represent it in another country

2.   Contractual Agreements

Licensing—Agreement in which one firm gives another firm the right to produce and market its product in a specified location in return for royalties.

Franchising—A form of licensing involving the right to adapt an entire system of doing business.

3.   Strategic Alliances—Relationship developed between a firm seeking a deeper commitment to a foreign market and a domestic firm in the target country.

Joint Venture—Strategic alliance in which a new entity owned by two or more firms is created to allow the partners to pool their resources for common goals.

4.   Direct Investment—When a firm expands internationally, buying a business outright in the host country, or building their own manufacturing or other operations.

B.   Product-Level Decisions: Choosing a Marketing Mix Strategy—It may or may not be necessary to develop a customized marketing mix for each country.

1.   Standardization versus Localization—Basic needs and wants are the same everywhere; or, each country has a national character with a distinctive set of behavioural and personality characteristics.

2.   Product Decisions—To sell a product in a foreign market there are three choices: a straight extension strategy, a product adaptation strategy, and a product invention strategy.

3.   Promotion Decisions—It may be necessary to change product promotions in a foreign market.

4.   Price Decisions—Costs associated with transportation, tariffs, and differences in currency exchange rates, etc. may affect the price abroad.

Grey Market—Unauthorized party imports products, then sells them for a fraction of the price.

Dumping—A company tries to get a toehold in a foreign market by pricing its products lower than they are offered at home.

5.   Distribution Decisions—A reliable distribution system is essential if the marketer is to succeed in a foreign market.

Key Terms   *Multiple Choice*

	Key Terms		Multiple Choice
1.	Trade flow	1.	a
2.	Competitive advantage	2.	b
3.	Demand conditions	3.	d
4.	Developing country	4.	a
5.	Economic communities	5.	b
6.	Political risk assessment	6.	c
7.	Nationalization	7.	d
8.	Protectionism	8.	d
9.	General Agreement of Tariffs & Trade (GATT)	9.	a
10.	Export merchants	10.	b
11.	Licensing	11.	a
12.	Franchising	12.	c
13.	Strategic alliance	13.	b
14.	Joint venture	14.	d
15.	Standardization	15.	a

Chapter in Review – Writing to Learn

1.   Firms choose to enter foreign markets for several reasons. The principle of comparative advantage means that each country should produce what it is best at. A country's market potential is based on its rate of population growth and economic conditions. A decline in domestic demand for particular products encourages some firms to look at foreign markets for growth.

2.   A country's stage of economic development determines a global firm's marketing opportunities. In less developed countries with subsistence economies, opportunities are usually limited to staples and inexpensive discretionary items. In developing countries, such as those in Eastern Europe, Latin America, and the Pacific Rim, an industrial-based economy is evolving and the rising middle class creates great demand for basic consumer goods. Developed countries such as Japan have highly sophisticated marketing systems and offer almost limitless marketing opportunities for goods and services.

3.   Firms that operate in two or more countries can choose to standardize their marketing strategies—that is, use the same strategies in all countries—or to localize by adopting different strategies for each market. Proponents of standardization perspective focus on commonalities across countries. Supporters of the localization perspective seek to adapt to the national character of each country.

Case Analysis

1.   MTV Europe's initial marketing objectives were to raise awareness and build viewership.

2.   MTV Europe's initial approach to the market involved standardization, because there was no attempt made to adapt the program to the needs of the local market.

3.   The language barrier was a major barrier MTV faced in Europe.

4.   MTV Europe elected to make changes in 1) the product element by introducing local programming, and 2) in the promotion element by sponsoring local advertising.

CHAPTER 5

Marketing Information and Research: Analyzing the Business Environment

CHAPTER OVERVIEW

In reading this chapter we learned that a marketing information system (MIS) is a system for gathering, sorting, analyzing, storing and distributing relevant marketing information. Information included in the MIS may be primary data that is specifically collected and analyzed for a particular marketing need, or secondary data gathered for some purpose other than the current marketing need.

We also considered the research process that begins with defining the problem to be researched and choosing the type of research that will provide the needed information. Exploratory research may be necessary to identify specific questions or issues, which can be addressed through problem-solving research. Good research methodology will ensure data that are reliable, valid, and representative of the population of interest. In addition, we addressed the importance of marketing research to firms in a global marketplace, where barriers to conducting marketing research may be related to the infrastructure of a country, translation problems, and legal restrictions.

Finally, in this chapter we reviewed the variety of research techniques available to marketers: exploratory research, problem-solving research, causal problem-solving research, and descriptive research. We concluded that the true value of research to the firm is in how marketers *implement* the research results.

CHAPTER OBJECTIVES

1. Describe the marketing research process.

2. Understand the differences among exploratory, problem-solving, and causal research, and describe some research techniques available to marketers.

3. Deal with the issues involved in making sense of research results.

4. Discuss how marketers implement research results.

CHAPTER OUTLINE

With reference to the textbook, please provide a brief description of each of the main elements listed in the Chapter Outline below. The page numbers will help guide you through the learning process.

I.   INFORMATION FOR DECISION MAKING _____ *(p.122)*
     Marketing Research _____ *(p.122)*
     A.   Information Needs
          1.   Ongoing Information _____ *(p.122)*
          2.   Monitored Information _____ *(p.122)*
          3.   Specific Information _____ *(p.123)*

II.   THE STEPS IN MARKETING RESEARCH
     A.   Defining the Problem_____ *(p.123)*
          1.   Specifying the Research Objectives _____ *(p.124)*
          2.   Identifying the Consumer Population of Interest ____ *(p.124)*
          3.   Placing the Problem in an Environmental Context ___ *(p.124)*

     B.   Determining the Research Technique
     Research Design _____ *(p.124)*
          1.   Exploratory Research _____ *(p.125)*
          Consumer Interviews _____ *(p.126)*
          Focus Group _____ *(p.126)*
          Projective Techniques _____ *(p.127)*
          Case Study_____ *(p.127)*
          Ethnography _____ *(p.127)*
          2.   Descriptive Research_____ *(p.128)*
          Cross-Sectional Design_____ *(p.128)*
          Longitudinal Design _____ *(p.129)*
          Survey _____ *(p.129)*
          3.   Causal Research _____ *(p.132)*
          Experiments _____ *(p.132)*

     C.   Gathering Data
     Secondary Data _____ *(p.133)*
     Primary Data _____ *(p.133)*
          1.   Gathering Data Internationally _____ *(p.133)*
          2.   Searching for the Pot of Gold:
          Single Source Data and Data Mining
          Single-Source Data _____ *(p.134)*
          Data Mining _____ *(p.135)*

D.   Ensuring the Quality of the Research: Garbage In, Garbage Out
    1.   Validity _____ *(p.135)*
    2.   Reliability _____ *(p.136)*
    3.   Representativeness _____ *(p.136)*
        Sampling _____ *(p.136)*

E.   Implementing the Research Results_____ *(p.136)*
    1.   Integrating Feedback into Long-Term Planning_____ *(p.138)*
        Marketing Information System (MIS)_____ *(p.138)*
    2.   Predicting the Future_____ *(p.138)*
        Scenarios _____ *(p.138)*

KEY TERMS

Select the correct term for each definition and write it in the space provided.

Validity	Primary data
Marketing research	Representativeness
Research design	Causal research
Survey	Marketing information system (MIS)
Reliability	Exploratory research
Projective techniques	Focus group
Marketing intelligence	Single-source data
Experiment	

1.   _____   Procedure developed by a firm to continuously gather, sort, analyze, store, and distribute relevant and timely marketing information to its managers. *(p.138)*

2.   _____   Information about a firm's external environment, which allows marketers to monitor conditions that affect demand for existing products or create demand for new products. *(p.122)*

3.   _____   Data collected for the specific purposes of the study. *(p.133)*

4.   _____   The process of collecting, analyzing, and interpreting data about customers, competitors, and the business environment to improve marketing effectiveness. *(p.122)*

5. _____ Information that is integrated from multiple sources to monitor the impact of marketing communications on a particular customer group over time. *(p.134)*

6. _____ Technique that marketers use to generate insights for future, more rigorous studies. *(p.125)*

7. _____ The extent to which research measurement techniques are free of errors. *(p.136)*

8. _____ The extent to which marketing research actually measures what it was intended to measure. *(p.135)*

9. _____ The extent to which consumers in a study are similar to a larger group in which the organization has an interest. *(p.136)*

10. _____ A plan that specifies what information marketers will collect and what type of study they will do. *(p.125)*

11. _____ A product-oriented discussion among a small group of consumers led by a trained moderator. *(p.126)*

12. _____ Tests that marketers use to explore people's underlying feelings about a product, especially appropriate when consumers are unable or unwilling to express true feelings. *(p.127)*

13. _____ Techniques that attempt to understand cause-and-effect relationships. *(p.132)*

14. _____ Techniques that test prespecified relationships among variables in a controlled environment. *(p.132)*

15. _____ A questionnaire that asks participants about their beliefs or behaviours. *(p.129)*

MULTIPLE CHOICE

Identify the most correct answer.

1.   Information that is needed to make smart decisions is: *(p.122-123)*
     a.   ongoing Information.
     b.   monitored Information.
     c.   specific Information.
     d.   all of the above.

2.   Data used by marketing, but gathered for some purpose other than a current marketing information need is called: *(p.133)*
     a.   outside data.
     b.   secondary data.
     c.   miscellaneous data.
     d.   primary data.

3.   A survey is: *(p.129)*
     a.   a questionnaire asking participants about their beliefs or behaviours.
     b.   published research on the state of the industry conducted by trade organizations.
     c.   data obtained from Statistics Canada.
     d.   all of the above.

4.   A research technique used by market researchers that tracks the responses of the same sample of respondents over time is a(n): *(p.129)*
     a.   form of descriptive research.
     b.   longitudinal design.
     c.   cross-sectional design.
     d.   customized survey.

5.   Defining the problem to be addressed by the research has the following component(s): *(p.124)*
     a.   specifying the research objectives.
     b.   identifying the consumer population of interest.
     c.   placing the problem in an environmental context.
     d.   all of the above.

6.   Causal research: *(p.132)*
     a.   investigates or explores a marketing problem that is not yet well-defined.
     b.   provides qualitative data, where the researcher collects data that add "personality and character" to descriptions of consumers' attitudes, feelings, and buying behaviours.
     c.   attempt to understand cause-and-effect relationships.
     d.   is relatively flexible and unstructured to allow researchers to follow-up on each consumer's unique responses in depth.

7. Using whomever is available and willing to participate in the research study is called: *(p.136)*
    a. convenience sampling.
    b. quota sampling
    c. random sampling.
    d. systematic sampling.

8. Sophisticated analysis techniques used by firms to take advantage of the massive amount of transaction information that is now available is known as: *(p.135)*
    a. sugging.
    b. Pot of Gold.
    c. data mining.
    d. search-soliciting.

9. The extent to which research measurement techniques are free from errors is: *(p.136)*
    a. reliability.
    b. validity.
    c. representativeness.
    d. consistency.

10. A product-oriented discussion among a small group of consumers led by a trained moderator is: *(p.126)*
    a. a product testing group.
    b. a focus group.
    c. an omnibus survey.
    d. random sampling.

11. Back-translation: *(p.134)*
    a. is a process used by many researchers trying to minimize the problems associated with mistranslation of a language.
    b. requires a questionnaire to be translated into a second language by a native speaker of that language.
    c. requires the new version of the questionnaire to be translated back into the original language.
    d. all of the above.

12. A detailed report on observations of people in their own homes and communities is called: *(p.127)*
    a. a case study.
    b. ethnography.
    c. a focus group.
    d. demography.

13. A type of problem-solving research that probes systematically into a problem and bases its conclusions on large numbers of observations is: *(p.128)*
   a. a case study.
   b. field research.
   c. descriptive research.
   d. hypothesizing.

14. A descriptive research technique that relies on nonhuman devices to record behaviour is called: *(p.131)*
   a. mechanical observation.
   b. cross-sectional design.
   c. a Likert scale.
   d. longitudinal design.

15. Data-collection methods used in descriptive research studies that rely on use of a passive instrument in which consumers are simply recorded include: *(p.130)*
   a. personal observation.
   b. unobtrusive measures.
   c. mechanical observation.
   d. all of the above.

CHAPTER IN REVIEW—WRITING TO LEARN

1. Discuss some of the issues marketers face when conducting marketing research.

_____

_____

_____

_____

2. Describe some of the research techniques available to marketers.

_____

_____

_____

_____

3.   Discuss how marketers implement research results.

_____

_____

_____

_____

CASE ANALYSIS

Real People, Real Decisions: Meet Dr. Marshall Rice, Surveysite

Reread the three sections comprising the Surveysite vignette in Chapter 5 and answer the following questions:

1.   What types of marketing decisions is Surveysite's research used to support?

2.   Describe how an online focus group is conducted.

3.   What type of sample did Dr. Rice use to find out whether his existing clients would be interested in online focus groups?

4.   Which advantages of online focus groups were identified by Surveysite's clients?

SCENARIO

You are Director of Marketing Research for a Canadian mutual fund company. There are more than 1000 mutual funds in Canada. Your company offers thirty different funds, with names like Equity Fund, Balanced Fund, Bond Fund, Mortgage Fund, and so forth.

The Director of Marketing at your firm has been considering renaming the funds to better reflect the goals and objectives of the customers who invest in them, e.g., Midlife Sabbatical Fund. She comes to you asking for advice on how to proceed.

1.   As a marketing researcher, how would you define the Director of Marketing's problem?
2.   What secondary data will you suggest be collected at the outset?
3.   Which exploratory research techniques will you recommend to generate fund names?
4.   Which descriptive research techniques will you recommend to ensure the new names accurately reflect the goals and objectives of your company's investors?

ANSWERS

Chapter Outline

I.   INFORMATION FOR DECISION MAKING—Business firms succeed by knowing what consumers want, when they want it, where they want it—and what competing firms are doing about it.
Marketing Research—The process of collecting, analyzing, and interpreting data about customers, competitors, and the business environment in order to improve marketing effectiveness.

     A.   Information Needs

          1.   Ongoing Information—Marketing managers use daily or weekly sales data to measure progress toward sales goals and market share objectives.

          2.   Monitored Information—Also called marketing intelligence, is information about a firm's external environment, which allows marketers to monitor conditions that affect demand for existing products or create demand for new products.

          3.   Specific Information—Marketing managers use immediate feedback, or specific information to identify opportunities for new products, etc.

II.   THE STEPS IN MARKETING RESEARCH

     A.   Defining the Problem—Defining the research problem as precisely as possible allows marketers to search for the right answers to the right questions. The three components include:

          1.   Specifying the Research Objectives—Which questions will the research attempt to answer?

          2.   Identifying the Consumer Population of Interest—What are the characteristics of the consumers involved in the problem situation?

          3.   Placing the Problem in an Environmental Context—Which factors in the firm's internal and external business environment might be influencing the situation?

     B.   Determining the Research Technique
Research Design—A plan that specifies what information will be collected and what type of study will be done.

          1.   Exploratory Research—A technique used by marketers to generate insights for future, more rigorous studies.
Consumer Interviews—One-on-one discussions between a consumer and a researcher.
Focus Group—A product-oriented discussion among a small group of consumers led by a trained moderator.
Projective Techniques—Tests used by marketers to explore people's underlying feelings about a product, especially appropriate when consumers are unable or unwilling to express their true reactions.
Case Study—A comprehensive examination of a particular firm or organization.
Ethnography—A detailed report based on observations of people in their own homes or communities.

          2.   Descriptive Research—A tool used by marketers that probes more systematically into the problem and bases its conclusions on large numbers of observations.
Cross-Sectional Design—A type of descriptive technique used by marketers that involves the systematic collection of quantitative information at one point in time.
Longitudinal Design—A technique used by market researchers that tracks the responses of the same sample of respondents over time.
Survey—A questionnaire used by market researchers that asks participants about their beliefs or behaviours. The different types include: Mail, Telephone, Face-to-Face, Online, Personal Observation, Unobtrusive Measures and Mechanical Observation.

          3.   Causal Research—Techniques that attempt to understand cause-and-effect relationships.
Experiments—Techniques used by researchers that test prespecified relationships among variables in a controlled environment.

C.   Gathering Data
Secondary Data—The purchase of existing data or data that has been collected by other organizations such as Statistics Canada's census data.
Primary Data—Collected for the specific purposes of the study.
1.   Gathering Data Internationally—Market conditions and consumer preferences vary widely in different parts of the world, and there are big differences in the sophistication of market research operations and the amount of data available to global marketers.
2.   Searching for the Pot of Gold: Single Source Data and Data Mining.
Single-Source Data—Information that is integrated from multiple sources, to monitor the impact of marketing communications on a particular customer group over time.
Data Mining—Sophisticated analysis techniques used by firms to take advantage of the massive amount of transaction information now available. Four important applications are: customer acquisition, customer retention, customer abandonment, and market basket analysis.

D.   Ensuring the Quality of the Research: Garbage In, Garbage Out
1.   Validity—The extent to which research actually measures what it was intended to measure.
2.   Reliability—The extent to which research measurement techniques are free of errors.
3.   Representativeness—The extent to which consumers in a study are similar to a larger group in which the organization has an interest.
Sampling—The process of selecting respondents who statistically represent a larger population of interest. Specific techniques include: Random sampling, a quota sample, and a convenience sample.

E.   Implementing the Research Results—The preparation of a report of the research results and their integration into long-term planning.
1.   Integrating Feedback into Long-Term Planning—Marketing research is an ongoing process of collecting and interpreting information that should be constantly referred to and updated as the company conducts long-term planning.
Marketing Information System (MIS)—A procedure developed by a firm to continuously gather, sort, analyze, store, and distribute relevant and timely marketing information to its managers.
2.   Predicting the Future—Futurists try to imaging different scenarios, or possible future situations.
Scenarios—Imagining possible future situations and assigning a level of probability to each.

Key Terms		*Multiple Choice*	
1.	Marketing Information System (MIS)	1.	d
2.	Marketing intelligence	2.	b
3.	Primary data	3.	a
4.	Marketing research	4.	b
5.	Single-source data	5.	d
6.	Exploratory research	6.	c
7.	Reliability	7.	a
8.	Validity	8.	c
9.	Representativeness	9.	a
10.	Research design	10.	b
11.	Focus group	11.	d
12.	Projective techniques	12.	b
13.	Causal research	13.	c
14.	Experiment	14.	a
15.	Survey	15.	d

Chapter in Review — Writing to Learn

1. The continued ability of marketing researchers to collect information is strongly tied to ethical research issues including deceptive practices of unscrupulous marketers, privacy issues, and special ethical concerns in conducting research with children. When operating in a global marketplace, barriers to conducting marketing research may be related to the infrastructure of a country, translation problems, and legal restrictions.

2. Exploratory research seeks qualitative data through such techniques as individual interviews, focus groups, projective techniques, and observational techniques such as ethnography. Causal research seeks to identify the cause or reason why something occurs and requires designing laboratory or field research experiments which can test pre-specified relationships. Descriptive studies may attempt to describe an issue or problem at one point in time (cross-sectional design) or over time (longitudinal design).

3. In order for research data to be useful to marketers, it must be sorted, organized and analyzed. How data are handled is influenced by the research method (exploratory, causal, cross-sectional, longitudinal, and so on), how the data are collected (phone, mail, or personal interview), and the types of questions asked (open-ended versus closed response). Effective marketing managers see research as an ongoing problem-solving process that must be constantly referred to and updated.

Case Analysis

1. Surveysite provides data that assists its clients with marketing decisions such as: the look and design of a company's Web site, which products and services to offer customers, how to provide better customer service, and what to charge for a company's products.

2. A group discussion would take place in an Internet chat room. Group participants would be invited to a Web site that would allow them to participate in focus group discussions on their own time over a specified period. Like a traditional focus group, an online focus group would be led by a trained moderator, who would monitor the online discussions and keep participants on track.

3. Dr. Rice used a convenience sample—he interviewed a small sample of his most important clients.

4. Interviewed clients mentioned several benefits of online focus groups, including: worldwide scope, ability to get results quickly, anonymity of the online environment, and the ability to deal more effectively with group domination issues.

CHAPTER 6

Why People Buy: Consumer Behaviour

CHAPTER OVERVIEW

The purpose of this chapter was to gain a better understanding of factors that influence consumer buying behaviour. Specifically, we considered a number of internal factors that influence consumer behaviour including perception, motivation and learning. We also examined how a consumer's attitude, which is a lasting evaluation of a person, object, or issue, can affect what they buy.

We reviewed other factors that influence consumer purchasing decisions and buying behaviour including personal, social, and situational issues. The personal influences on consumers are important determinants of their needs and wants. Such factors as age, income, family status, and chosen lifestyle are strongly related to the types of products people buy and the specific brands they select.

We examined the stages of the consumer decision-making process: problem recognition, information search, evaluation of alternatives, product choice and postpurchase evaluation. We also addressed the impact of the amount of effort expended and of perceived risk, factors associated with relative importance and perceived consequences of the purchase, from the consumer's perspective.

CHAPTER OBJECTIVES

1. Explain why understanding consumer behaviour is important to organizations.

2. Explain the prepurchase, purchase, and postpurchase activities consumers engage in when making decisions.

3. Describe how internal factors influence consumers' decision making processes.

4. Understand how situational factors can influence consumer behaviour.

5. Describe how consumers' relationships with other people influence their decision making processes.

CHAPTER OUTLINE

With reference to the textbook, please provide a brief description of each of the main elements listed in the Chapter Outline below. The page numbers will help guide you through the learning process.

I.   DECISIONS, DECISIONS
    Consumer Behaviour _____ *(p.146)*
    Involvement _____ *(p.147)*
    Perceived Risk _____ *(p.147)*
    A.   Problem Recognition _____ *(p.148)*
    B.   Information Search _____ *(p.148)*
    C.   Evaluation of Alternatives
        Evaluation Criteria _____ *(p.149)*
    D.   Product Choice
        Heuristics _____ *(p.149)*
        Brand Loyalty _____ *(p.149)*
    E.   Postpurchase Evaluation
        Customer Satisfaction/Dissatisfaction _____ *(p.149)*

II.   INTERNAL INFLUENCES ON CONSUMER DECISIONS
    A.   Perception _____ *(p.151)*
        Exposure _____ *(p.151)*
        Perceptual Selection _____ *(p.152)*
        Interpretations _____ *(p.152)*
    B.   Motivation _____ *(p.152)*
        Hierarchy of Needs _____ *(p.152)*
    C.   Learning _____ *(p.153)*
        1.   Behavioural Learning
            Behavioural Learning Theories _____ *(p.153)*
            Classical Conditioning _____ *(p.153)*
            Operant Conditioning _____ *(p.153)*
            Stimulus Generalization _____ *(p.153)*
        2.   Cognitive Learning
            Cognitive Learning Theory _____ *(p.154)*
    D.   Attitudes _____ *(p.154)*
    E.   Personality _____ *(p.154)*
        Innovativeness _____ *(p.155)*
        Self-Confidence _____ *(p.155)*
        Sociability _____ *(p.155)*
        Self-Concept _____ *(p.155)*
    F.   Age Groups
        Family Life Cycle _____ *(p.157)*
    G.   Lifestyles
        Lifestyle _____ *(p.158)*
        Psychographics _____ *(p.158)*

III. SITUATIONAL INFLUENCES ON CONSUMER DECISIONS
    A. Physical Environment _____ *(p.159)*
    B. Time_____ *(p.159)*

IV. SOCIAL INFLUENCES ON CONSUMER DECISIONS
    A. Culture_____ *p. 161)*
    B. Subcultures _____ *(p.162)*
    C. Social Class _____ *(p.162)*
       Status Symbols _____ *(p.162)*
    D. Group Behaviour
       1. Reference Group _____ *(p.164)*
          Conformity _____ *(p.164)*
          Sex Roles_____ *(p.164)*
       2. Opinion Leaders
          Opinion Leader _____ *(p.165)*

KEY TERMS

Select the correct term for each definition and write it in the space provided.

Learning
Social class
Consumer behaviour
Opinion leader
Evaluative criteria
Personality
Culture
Brand loyalty

Exposure
Subculture
Attitude
Motivation
Involvement
Perception
Family lifecycle

1. _____ The processes involved when individuals or groups select, purchase and use goods, services, ideas, or experiences to satisfy needs and desires. *(p.146)*

2. _____ The process by which people select, organize, and interpret information from the outside world. *(p.151)*

3. _____ The degree to which a marketing stimulus is within range of consumer's sensory receptors. *(p.151)*

4. _____ A pattern of repeat product purchases, accompanied by an underlying positive attitude toward the brand, which is based on the belief that the brand makes products superior to its competition. *(p.149)*

5. _____ An internal state that drives us to satisfy needs by activating goal-oriented behaviour. *(p.152)*

6. _____ A relatively permanent change in behaviour that is caused by experience or acquired information. *(p.153)*

7. _____ A learned predisposition to respond favourably or unfavourably to stimuli, based on relatively enduring evaluations of people, objects, and issues. *(p.154)*

8. _____ The psychological characteristics that consistently influence the way a person responds to situations in the environment. *(p.154)*

9. _____ A means of characterizing consumers based on different family stages they pass through as they grow older. *(p.157)*

10. _____ The values, beliefs, customs, and tastes that a group of people value. *(p.160)*

11. _____ The overall rank or social standing of groups of people within a society according to the value assigned to such factors as family background, education, occupation, and income. *(p.162)*

12. _____ A person who is frequently able to influence others' attitudes or behaviours by virtue of their active interest and expertise in one or more product categories. *(p.165)*

13. _____   A group within a society whose members
                                share a distinctive set of beliefs,
                                characteristics, or common experiences.
                                (p.162)

14. _____   The relative importance of the perceived
                                consequences of the purchase to a consumer.
                                (p.147)

15. _____   The dimensions that consumers use to
                                compare competing product alternatives.
                                (p.148)

MULTIPLE CHOICE

Identify the most correct answer.

1. The stimulus that must be within range of people's sensory receptors to be noticed is called: *(p.151)*
    a. perceptual selectivity.
    b. exposure.
    c. sensory overload.
    d. adaptation.

2. Learning that occurs as the result of rewards or punishments is called: *(p.153)*
    a. attitude conditioning.
    b. behavioural conditioning.
    c. classical conditioning.
    d. operant conditioning.

3. According to Abraham Maslow's Theory of Motivation, there exists a/an: *(p.153)*
    a. hierarchy of needs.
    b. conscience.
    c. referee in the subconscious struggle between temptation and virtue.
    d. opposing force to the superid.

4. According to Maslow's Hierarchy of Needs, the need(s) at the lowest level of importance is/are: *(p.153)*
    a. spiritual fulfillment.
    b. food, clothing, and shelter.
    c. social approval.
    d. a sense of family.

5.	Theories of learning that stress the importance of internal mental processes and that view people as problem-solvers who actively use information from the world around them to master their environment are known as: *(p.154)*
	a.	behavioural learning theories.
	b.	classical conditioning.
	c.	cognitive learning theories.
	d.	positive reinforcement.

6.	The three components of attitude are: *(p.154)*
	a.	innovativeness, self confidence and sociability.
	b.	personality, self concept and lifestyle.
	c.	behavioural, classical and operant.
	d.	affect, cognition and behaviour.

7.	Self concept is: *(p.155)*
	a.	an individual's self-image that is composed of a mixture of beliefs, observations, and feelings about personal attributes.
	b.	the degree to which a person has a positive evaluation of his/her abilities.
	c.	the degree to which a person enjoys social interaction.
	d.	none of the above.

8.	The pattern of living that determines how people choose to spend their time, money, and energy and that reflects their values, tastes, and preferences is called: *(p.158)*
	a.	life cycle.
	b.	personality.
	c.	lifestyle.
	d.	self-esteem.

9.	A group within a society whose members share a distinctive set of beliefs, characteristics, or common experiences is a: *(p.162)*
	a.	social class.
	b.	subculture.
	c.	reference group.
	d.	norm.

10.	An actual or imaginary individual or group that has a significant effect on an individual's evaluations, aspirations and behaviour is called: *(p.164)*
	a.	an opinion leader.
	b.	a subculture.
	c.	a reference group.
	d.	a status symbol.

11. The importance of perceived consequences of a purchase to a consumer is called: *(p.147)*
    a. involvement.
    b. perceived risk.
    c. attitude.
    d. all of the above.

12. A product that is purchased to signal membership in a desirable social class is a: *(p.162)*
    a. subculture.
    b. social class.
    c. culture.
    d. status symbol.

13. The process whereby the consumer checks his or her memory and/or surveys his or her environment in order to collect the data required to make a reasonable decision is: *(p.148)*
    a. problem recognition.
    b. information search.
    c. perceived risk.
    d. habitual decision making.

14. A change in beliefs or actions as a reaction to real or imagined group pressure is called: *(p.164)*
    a. opinion leadership.
    b. an inference group.
    c. conformity.
    d. a social class.

15. Example(s) of heuristics include: *(p.149)*
    a. the belief that price equals quality.
    b. brand loyalty.
    c. mental shortcuts that lead to a speedy decision.
    d. all of the above.

CHAPTER IN REVIEW—WRITING TO LEARN

1. Discuss the role perception plays in influencing consumer behaviour.

_____

_____

_____

_____

2.   Identify the factors that influence purchasing decisions and buyer behaviour.

_____

_____

_____

_____

3.   Discuss the role motivation plays, as a factor that can influence consumer behaviour.

_____

_____

_____

_____

CASE ANALYSIS

Real People, Real Decisions: Robert Barnard, d~Code

Reread the three sections comprising the d~Code vignette in Chapter 6 and answer the following questions:

1.   Who is the Nexus generation, and why is this segment important to Canadian marketers?

2.   What did the research reveal about important distinguishing characteristics of Nexus buyers?

3.   Which lifestyle elements distinguish Nexus consumers from the rest of the Canadian population?

4.   How can insight into Nexus buying behaviour help d~Code's customers with marketing decisions?

SCENARIO

You are the Director of Marketing for a major car company. Your company has recently launched an inexpensive sport utility vehicle (SUV) whose target market is 18-29 year olds, earning $25,000 to $40,000 annually. You have been asked to speak at a convention of auto dealership owners. The dealers want to gain a better understanding of how this segment buys automobiles, and your boss has asked you to address the following questions in your presentation:

1.   How does this segment conduct an information search—where do they seek information about SUVs?
2.   What are this segment's evaluative criteria—on what basis do they evaluate the relative merits of SUVs?
3.   Which of Maslow's needs is this segment attempting to fulfill through the purchase of an SUV?
4.   Which situational and social influences have an impact on this segment's car purchasing decisions?

ANSWERS

Chapter Outline

I.   DECISIONS, DECISIONS
     Consumer Behaviour—The process individuals or groups go through to select, purchase, and use goods, services, ideas or experiences to satisfy their needs and desires.
     Involvement—The relative importance of perceived consequences of the purchase to a consumer.
     Perceived Risk—The belief that use of a product has potentially negative consequences, either financial, physical or social.
     A.   Problem Recognition—Occurs whenever the consumer sees a significant difference between his or her current state of affairs and some desired or ideal state; this recognition initiates the decision-making process.
     B.   Information Search—The process whereby a consumer searches for appropriate information to make a reasonable decision.
     C.   Evaluation of Alternatives
          Evaluative Criteria—Dimensions used by consumers to compare competing product alternatives.
     D.   Product Choice
          Heuristics—A mental rule of thumb that leads to a speedy decision by simplifying the process.
          Brand Loyalty—A pattern of repeat product purchases, accompanied by an underlying positive attitude toward the brand, which is based on the belief that the brand makes products superior to its competition.
     E.   Postpurchase Evaluation
          Consumer Satisfaction/Dissatisfaction—The overall feelings or attitude a person has about a product after purchasing it.

II. INTERNAL INFLUENCES ON CONSUMER DECISIONS
     A.   Perception—The process by which people select, organize and interpret information from the outside world.
          Exposure—The stimulus that must be within range of people's sensory receptors to be noticed.
          Perceptual Selection—Consumers choose to pay some attention to some stimuli but not to others.
          Interpretation—Meaning that is assigned to stimulus.
     B.   Motivation—An internal state that drives us to satisfy needs by activating goal-oriented behaviour.
          Hierarchy of Needs—An   approach that categorizes motives according to five levels of importance, the more basic needs being on the bottom of the hierarchy and the higher needs at the top.
     C.   Learning—A relatively permanent change in the behaviour caused by acquired information or experience.
          1.   Behavioural Learning
               Behavioural Learning Theories—Theories of learning that focus on how consumer behaviour is changed by external events or stimuli.
               Classical Conditioning—The learning that occurs when the stimulus eliciting a response is paired with another stimulus that initially does not elicit a response on its own but will cause a similar response over time because of its association with the first stimulus.
               Operant Conditioning—Learning that occurs as the result of rewards or punishments.
               Stimulus Generalization—Behaviour caused by a reaction to one stimulus that occurs in the presence of another, similar stimulus.
          2.   Cognitive Learning
               Cognitive Learning Theory—The theory of learning that stresses the importance of internal mental processes and that view people as problem-solvers who actively use information from the world around them to master their environment.
     D.   Attitude—A learned predisposition to respond favourably or unfavourably to stimuli based on relatively enduring evaluations of people, objects, and issues.

E. Personality—The psychological characteristics that consistently influence the way a person responds to situations in the environment.

Innovativeness—The degree to which a person likes to try new things.

Self-Confidence—The degree to which a person has a positive evaluation of his or her own abilities.

Sociability—The degree to which a person enjoys social interaction.

Self-Concept—An individual's self-image that is composed of a mixture of beliefs, observations, and feelings about personal attributes.

F. Age Groups

Family Life Cycle—A means of characterizing based on the different family stages people pass through as they grow older.

G. Lifestyles

Lifestyle—The pattern of living that determines how people choose to spend their time, money, and energy that reflects their values, tastes, and preferences.

Psychographics—Information about the activities, interests and opinions of consumers that is used to construct market segments.

III. SITUATIONAL INFLUENCES ON CONSUMER DECISIONS

A. Physical Environment—The impact of in-store displays and place-based media.

B. Time—Consumers' reactions to marketing innovations that help them save time.

IV. SOCIAL INFLUENCES ON CONSUMER DECISIONS

A. Culture—The values, beliefs and tastes valued by a group of people.

B. Subculture—A group within a society whose members share a distinctive set of beliefs, characteristics or common experience.

C. Social Class—The overall rank or social standing of groups of people within a society according to the value assigned to such factors as family background, education, occupation and income.

Status Symbol—Products that are purchased to signal membership in a desirable social class.

D. Group Behaviour

1. Reference Group—An actual or imaginary individual or group that has a significant effect on an individual's evaluation's, aspirations or behaviour.

Conformity—A change in beliefs or actions as a reaction to real or imagined group pressure.

Sex Roles—Society's expectations regarding the appropriate attitude, behaviours and appearance for men and women.

2. Opinion Leaders

Opinion Leader—A person who is frequently able to influence others' attitudes or behaviours by virtue of their active interests and expertise in one or more product categories.

Key Terms

1. Consumer behaviour
2. Perception
3. Exposure
4. Brand loyalty
5. Motivation
6. Learning
7. Attitude
8. Personality
9. Family lifecycle
10. Culture
11. Social class
12. Opinion leader
13. Subculture
14. Involvement
15. Evaluative criteria

Multiple Choice

1. b
2. d
3. a
4. b
5. c
6. d
7. a
8. c
9. b
10. c
11. a
12. d
13. b
14. c
15. d

Chapter in Review—Writing to Learn

1. Perception is the process by which consumers select, organize and interpret the marketing stimuli to which they are exposed. To prevent sensory overload, consumers practice perceptual selectivity by choosing which stimuli they will pay attention to and which they will ignore.

2. Consumer purchasing decisions and buying behaviour are influenced by many factors that include personal, social, and situational issues. The personal influences on consumers are important determinants of their needs and wants. Such factors as age, income, family status, and chosen lifestyle are strongly related to the types of products people buy and the specific brands they want.

3. Motivation is an internal state that drives us to satisfy needs. Once we activate a need, a state of tension exists that drives the consumer toward some goal that will reduce this tension by eliminating the need.

Case Analysis

1. The Nexus generation is defined as 18-34 year old Canadians. They are attractive to marketers because they account for approximately one third of the Canadian adult population.

2. In terms of buying behaviour, the Nexus segment can be described as experimental and less brand loyal than other people, although they are willing to develop loyalty to brands that can offer a strong identity that is consistent with their values. They view buying as fun, and are confident in their abilities as shoppers, but are wary of flashy marketing campaigns.

3. Lifestyle elements that distinguish the Nexus consumers from other segments of the population include a greater interest in leisure activities, such as movies and amusement parks, and an embracing of extreme sports, such as skateboarding, rock climbing and snowboarding. They are also the most well-travelled young generation to date.

4. Insight into the Nexus segment can assist marketers with a wide range of marketing decisions including new product development, advertising approach, and design of the retail environment.

CHAPTER 7

Why Organizations Buy:
Business-to-Business Markets

CHAPTER OVERVIEW

In this chapter, we learned about the general characteristics of business-to-business markets and business buying practices. Business-to-business markets include business and organizational customers who buy goods and services for purposes other than for personal consumption. Business and organizational customers are usually few in number, may be geographically concentrated, and often purchase higher-priced products in larger quantities. Business buying practices include decisions regarding how a firm will utilize its suppliers, or sources, and which goods and services it needs. A firm's purchasing options include single sourcing, multiple sourcing, or systems buying.

Business and organizational markets are most frequently classified by the North American Industry Classification System (NAICS), a numerical coding system developed by NAFTA countries. More generally, business markets can be divided into the following major categories: producers, resellers, governments, and not-for-profit organizations.

Next, we reviewed how the business buy class reflects the degree and effort required to make a business buying decision. Purchase situations can involve a straight rebuy, modified rebuy, or new-task buying. A buying centre is a group of people who work together to make a buying decision. The roles in the buying centre are initiator, user, gatekeeper, influencer, decider, and buyer. The most important change in business buying is the growth of electronic commerce or e-commerce in which firms buy and sell products using the Internet, intranets, or extranets.

Lastly, the business buying decision process involves a number of stages that are similar, but more complex, than the steps followed by consumers when making a purchase decision. The recognition stage is accompanied by the submission of a purchase requisition and initiates the subsequent steps of developing product specifications, identifying potential suppliers, requesting and obtaining proposals, evaluating the proposals, selecting a supplier, placing the order, and finally, formal evaluation of the performance of the product and the supplier.

CHAPTER OBJECTIVES

1.   Describe the general characteristics of business-to-business markets and business buying practices.

2.   Explain how marketers classify business and organizational markets.

3.   Explain the business buying situation and describe business buyers.

4.   Summarize the stages in the business buying decision process.

5.   Explain how e-commerce is dramatically changing business-to-business marketing.

CHAPTER OUTLINE

With reference to the textbook, please provide a brief description of each of the main elements listed in the Chapter Outline below. The page numbers will help guide you through the learning process.

I.   BUSINESS MARKETS: BUYING AND SELLING WHEN STAKES ARE HIGH
        Business-To-Business Marketing _____ *(p.175)*
        A.   Characteristics That Make a Difference
                In Business Markets
                1.   Multiple Buyers_____ *(p.175)*
                2.   Number of Customers _____ *(p.176)*
                3.   Size of Purchases_____ *(p.176)*
                4.   Geographic Concentration _____ *(p.176)*
        B.   Business-to-Business Demand
                1.   Derived Demand _____ *(p.177)*
                2.   Inelastic Demand_____ *(p.178)*
                3.   Fluctuating Demand _____ *(p.179)*
                        Acceleration Principle_____ *(p.179)*
                4.   Joint Demand _____ *(p.179)*

II.   CLASSIFYING BUSINESS-TO-BUSINESS MARKETS _____ *(p.179)*
        North American Industry Classification System (NAICS) _____ *(p.180)*
        A.   Producers_____ *(p.181)*
        B.   Resellers _____ *(p.181)*
        C.   Governments
                Government Markets_____ *(p.181)*
                Competitive Bids _____ *(p.182)*
        D.   Not-For-Profit Institutions_____ *(p.183)*

III.   THE NATURE OF BUSINESS BUYING _____ *(p.183)*
        A.   The Buying Situation
                Buy Class_____ *(p.183)*
                1.   Straight Rebuy_____ *(p.183)*
                2.   Modified Rebuy _____ *(p.183)*
                3.   New-Task Buying_____ *(p.184)*

B.   The Professional Buyer
Centralized Purchasing _____ *(p.186)*
C.   The Buying Centre _____ *(p.187)*
    1.   The Fluid Nature of the Buying Centre
    2.   Roles in the Buying Centre
        Initiator _____ *(p.188)*
        User _____ *(p.188)*
        Gatekeeper _____ *(p.188)*
        Influencer _____ *(p.188)*
        Decider _____ *(p.188)*
        Buyer _____ *(p.188)*
D.   Electronic Business-To-Business Commerce
Electronic Commerce _____ *(p.189)*
Intranet _____ *(p.189)*

IV.   THE BUSINESS BUYING DECISION PROCESS
A.   Problem Recognition _____ *(p.190)*
B.   Information Search _____ *(p.190)*
    1.   Developing Product Specifications _____ *(p.191)*
    2.   Obtaining Proposals _____ *(p.191)*
C.   Evaluation of Alternatives _____ *(p.191)*
D.   Product and Supplier Selection _____ *(p.191)*
Just-In-Time (JIT) _____ *(p.191)*
Single Sourcing _____ *(p.192)*
Multiple Sourcing _____ *(p.192)*
Reciprocity _____ *(p.192)*
Outsourcing _____ *(p.192)*
Reverse Marketing _____ *(p.192)*
E.   Postpurchase Evaluation _____ *(p.192)*

KEY TERMS

Select the correct term for each definition and write it in the space provided.

Derived demand	Buyer
Buying centre	Reseller market
Not-for-profit institutions	Business and organizational customers
Outsourcing	Initiator
Competitive bids	Modified rebuy
Business-to-business marketing	Single sourcing
Just-in-time (JIT)	Centralized purchasing
North American Industry	
Classification System (NAICS)	

1. _____ Business firms and other organizations that buy goods and services for some purpose other than for personal consumption. *(p.174-175)*

2. _____ The marketing of goods and services that business and organizational customers need to produce other goods and services for resale and to support their operations. *(p.174)*

3. _____ Demand for business or organizational products derived from demand for consumer goods or services. *(p.177)*

4. _____ The business practice of buying a particular product from only one supplier. *(p.192)*

5. _____ The business buying practice of obtaining outside vendors to provide goods or services that otherwise might be supplied in-house. *(p.192)*

6. _____ A business buying process in which two or more suppliers submit proposals (including price and associated data) for a proposed purchase and the firm providing the better offer gets the bid. *(p.182)*

7. _____ The numerical coding system that the United States, Canada, and Mexico use to classify firms into detailed categories according to their business activities and shared characteristics. *(p.180)*

8. _____ The individuals or organizations that buy finished goods for the purpose of reselling, renting, or leasing to others at a profit and for maintaining their business operations. *(p.181)*

9. _____ The organizations with charitable, educational, community, and other public-service goals that buy goods and services to support their functions and to attract and serve their members. *(p.182)*

10. _____ A business buying practice in which an organization's purchasing department does the buying for all of the company. *(p.186)*

11. _____ A buying situation classification used by business buyers to categorize a previously made purchase that involves some change and that requires limited decision making. *(p.183)*

12. _____ The group of people in an organization who influence and participate in particular purchasing decisions. *(p.189)*

13. _____ The member of a business buying centre who first recognizes that a purchase needs to be made and notifies others in the organization. *(p.188)*

14. _____ The member of a business buying centre who has the formal authority and responsibility for executing the purchase. *(p.188)*

15. _____ Inventory management and purchasing practices used by manufacturers and resellers that reduce inventory and stock to very low levels, but assure deliveries from suppliers arrive just when needed. *(p.191)*

MULTIPLE CHOICE

Identify the most correct answer.

1. Characteristic(s) of the business market that complicates the marketing process, and what makes these markets attractive in the first place, include: *(p.176-177)*
   a. the size of the market.
   b. the volume of purchases.
   c. the concentration of potential customers in specific geographic regions.
   d. all of the above.

2.   A small percentage change in consumer demand can create a large percentage change in total industrial or business demand, which is known as: *(p.179)*
   a.   the acceleration principle.
   b.   inelastic demand.
   c.   the ripple effect.
   d.   indirect marketing.

3.   Multiple sourcing is: *(p.192)*
   a.   when two or more goods are used together to manufacture a product.
   b.   the business practice of buying a particular product from several different suppliers.
   c.   acquiring specialized services from outside suppliers.
   d.   the business buying practice of obtaining outside vendors to provide goods or services that otherwise might be supplied "in-house".

4.   A business buying practice in which organizations simplify the decision process by buying a particular product from only one supplier is called: *(p.192)*
   a.   single sourcing.
   b.   outsourcing.
   c.   systems buying.
   d.   sampling buying.

5.   Inelastic demand: *(p.178)*
   a.   means that a buyer and seller agree to be each other's customers.
   b.   is a practice in which many of the functions of buyer and seller are reversed.
   c.   means the demand for products does not change because of increases or decreases in price.
   d.   none of the above.

6.   The internal computer connections that organizations use to distribute information among different offices and locations. *(p.189)*
   a.   e-mail.
   b.   Internet.
   c.   e-commerce.
   d.   Intranet.

7.   The federal, provincial and local governments that buy goods to support public objectives and to carry on their operations are known as: *(p.181)*
   a.   public markets.
   b.   government markets.
   c.   institutional markets.
   d.   community markets.

8. A buy class: *(p.183)*
   a. is identified by the degree of effort required to collect information and make a decision.
   b. is applied to three different buying situations.
   c. includes a straight rebuy, modified rebuy, and new-task buy.
   d. all of the above.

9. A buying situation classification used by business buyers to categorize routine purchases that require minimal decision making is a: *(p.183)*
   a. modified rebuy.
   b. new-task buy.
   c. straight rebuy.
   d. routine buy.

10. A new-task buy: *(p.183)*
    a. is a buying situation when a purchase is made for the very first time.
    b. is characterized by certainty and no risk.
    c. involves the least effort since the buyer has no previous experience on which to base a decision.
    d. all of the above.

11. A member of a business buying centre who will ultimately use the product is a(n): *(p.188)*
    a. initiator.
    b. decider.
    c. user.
    d. buyer.

12. The gatekeeper is the member of a business buying centre who: *(p.188)*
    a. gives purchasing expertise.
    b. controls the flow of information to other members.
    c. first recognizes that a purchase needs to be made.
    d. controls the distribution of products purchased.

13. A member of a business buying centre who affects the buying decision by dispensing advice or sharing expertise is called a(n): *(p.188)*
    a. influencer.
    b. buyer.
    c. initiator.
    d. mentor.

14. The decider: *(p.188)*
    a. is the member of the buying centre who makes the final decision.
    b. may have formal or informal power to authorize spending the company's money.
    c. may be the purchasing agent or the CEO of an organization.
    d. all of the above.

15. The buying and selling of products electronically, usually via the Internet, is called. *(p.189)*
    a.   centralized purchasing.
    b.   competitive bidding.
    c.   electronic commerce, or e-commerce.
    d.   cost analysis.

CHAPTER IN REVIEW—WRITING TO LEARN

1. Describe the general characteristics of business-to-business markets.

    _____

    _____

    _____

    _____

2. Identify the three major categories of business markets.

    _____

    _____

    _____

    _____

3. Describe the function of a buying centre in business buying behaviour.

    _____

    _____

    _____

    _____

CASE ANALYSIS

Real People, Real Decisions: Michel Bendayan, Ritvik Holdings Inc.

Reread the three sections comprising the Ritvik Holdings vignette in Chapter 7 and answer the following questions:

1.   What is the major NAICS code for Ritvik Holdings?

2.   According to Figure 7.3 in Chapter 7, how should Ritvik Holdings be classified, as a producer, reseller or organization?

3.   Is Ritvik Holdings involved in B2B or B2C marketing – who are the company's clients?

4.   What is the main concern of Ritvik's European clients?

SCENARIO

You are an Account Executive for a software company that sells mortgage systems to major banks. Your company's mortgage system accommodates customer data, stores information about the mortgage features selected, i.e., is it biweekly, monthly, etc. and provides the ability to calculate mortgage payments and interest and do "what if" scenarios, e.g., what if I made a lump sum payment of $10,000 on the first anniversary of my mortgage? The system also produces annual mortgages statements for each customer.

Your company has received a request for proposal (RFP) from a major financial institution. A meeting has been arranged with the Vice President, Mortgages of this institution, at which you will be expected to present the proposal. Others will be present at the meeting, but they have not been identified in advance.

To prepare yourself in advance of the meeting, you ponder the following questions:

1.   Who are the people in this organization that will participate in the decision making process, i.e., who is the buying centre?
2.   Which roles will the different people in the buying centre occupy in the decision process, and what can I do to address the concerns of each?
3.   How will the people present evaluate the alternative proposals, i.e., what are their buying criteria?
4.   What do I need to do, in advance of the meeting, to determine if there is an opportunity for reciprocity?

ANSWERS

Chapter Outline

I.   BUSINESS MARKETS: BUYING AND SELLING WHEN STAKES ARE HIGH
     Business-to-Business Marketing—Marketing of goods and services that business and organizational customers need to produce other goods and services for resale or to support their operations.
     A.   Characteristics That Make a Difference In Business Markets
          1.   Multiple Buyers—In business markets, products often have to do more than satisfy an individual's needs. They must meet the requirements of everyone involved in the company's purchase decision.
          2.   Number of Customers—Business marketers have a narrow customer base and a small number of buyers.
          3.   Size of Purchases—Business-to-Business products can dwarf consumer purchases, both in the quantity of items ordered and in the price of individual purchases.
          4.   Geographic Concentration—Many business customers are located in a small geographic area, rather than being spread out across the country. Firms often choose to set up shop in areas that allow easy access to their buyers and suppliers.

     B.   Business-To-Business Demand
          1.   Derived Demand—Demand for business or organizational products is derived from demand for consumer goods or services.
          2.   Inelastic Demand—Demand for products that does not change because of increases or decreases in price.
          3.   Fluctuating Demand—When talking about demand coming from the end consumer, even small changes can create large increases or decreases in business demand.
               Acceleration Principle—A marketing phenomenon in which a small percentage change in consumer demand can create a large percentage change in business-to-business demand.
          4.   Joint Demand—Demand for two or more goods that are used together to create a product.

II. CLASSIFYING BUSINESS-TO-BUSINESS MARKETS—Many firms buy products in business markets so they can produce other goods in turn.
     North American Industry Classification System (NAICS)—The numerical coding system that the United States, Canada, and Mexico use to classify industries into detailed categories according to their business activities and shared characteristics.
     A.   Producers—The individuals or organizations that purchase products for use in the production of other goods and services.
          B.   Resellers—The individuals or organizations that buy finished goods for the purpose of reselling, renting, or leasing to others to make a profit and to maintain their business operations.
     C.   Governments
          Government Markets—The federal, provincial and local governments that buy goods and services to carry out public objectives and to support their operations.
          Competitive Bids—A business buying process in which two or more suppliers submit proposals (including price and associated data) for a proposed purchase and the firm providing the better offer gets the bid.
     D.   Not-For-Profit Institutions—The organizations with charitable, educational, community, and other public service goals that buy goods and services to support their functions and to attract and serve their members.

III. THE NATURE OF BUSINESS BUYING—To be successful in business-to-business markets requires developing marketing strategies that meet the needs of organizational customers better than the competition.

A. The Buying Situation

Buy Class—One of three classifications of business buyers that characterizes the degree of time and effort required to make a decision in a buying situation.

    1. Straight Rebuy—A buying situation in which business buyers make routine purchases that require minimal decision making.

    2. Modified Rebuy—A buying situation classification used by business buyers to categorize a previously made purchase that involves some change and that requires limited decision making.

    3. New-Task Buying—A new business-to-business purchase that is complex or risky and that requires extensive decision making.

B. The Professional Buyer

Centralized Purchasing—A business buying practice in which an organization's purchasing department does the buying for all of the company.

C. The Buying Centre—The group of people in an organization that influences and participates in purchasing decisions.

    1. The Fluid Nature of the Buying Centre

    2. Roles in the Buying Centre

Initiator—Begins the buying process by first recognizing that the firm needs to make a purchase.

User—Is the member of the buying centre who needs the purchased product

Gatekeeper—Is the member who controls the flow of information to other members

Influencer—Affects the buying decision by dispensing advice or sharing expertise

Decider—Is the member of the buying centre who makes the final decision

Buyer—Is the person who has responsibility for executing the purchase

D. Electronic Business-To-Business Commerce

Electronic Commerce—The buying and selling of products electronically, usually via the Internet

Intranet—Internal computer connections that organizations use to distribute information among their different offices and locations.

IV. THE BUSINESS BUYING DECISION PROCESS

A. Problem Recognition—Occurs when someone sees that a purchase can solve a problem.

B. Information Search—Searching for information about products and suppliers.

    1. Developing Product Specifications—A written description laying out their exact product requirements-the quality size, weight, colour, etc.

    2. Obtaining Proposals—The buyer's next step is to obtain written or verbal proposals, or bids, from one or more potential suppliers.

C. Evaluation of Alternatives—This stage is when the buying centre assesses the proposals.

D. Product And Supplier Selection—The selection of the best product and supplier to meet the firm's needs.

Just-In-Time (JIT)—Inventory management and purchasing processes that manufacturers and resellers use to reduce inventory to very low levels and ensure that deliveries from suppliers arrive only when needed.

Single Sourcing—The business practice of buying a particular product from only one supplier.

Multiple Sourcing—The business practice of buying a particular product from many suppliers.

Outsourcing—The business buying process of obtaining outside vendors to provide goods or services that otherwise might be supplied in-house.

Reverse Marketing—A business practice in which a buyer firm shapes a supplier's products and operations to satisfy its needs.

E. Postpurchase Evaluation—An organizational buyer assesses whether the performance of the product and the supplier is living up to expectations.

Key Terms

1. Business and organizational customers
2. Business-to-business marketing
3. Derived demand
4. Single sourcing
5. Outsourcing
6. Competitive bids
7. North American Industry Classification System (NAICS)
8. Reseller market
9. Not-For-Profit Institutions
10. Centralized purchasing
11. Modified rebuy
12. Buying centre
13. Initiator
14. Buyer
15. Just-in-time (JIT)

Multiple Choice

1. d
2. a
3. b
4. a
5. c
6. d
7. b
8. d
9. c
10. a
11. c
12. b
13. a
14. d
15. c

Chapter in Review—Writing to Learn

1. Business-to-business markets include business and organizational customers that buy goods and services for purposes other than for personal consumption. Business and organizational customers are usually few in number, may be geographically concentrated, and often purchase higher priced products in larger quantities.

2. Business markets can be divided into three major categories: producers, resellers, and organizations. Producers purchase materials, parts, and various goods and services needed to produce other goods and services to be sold at a profit. Resellers purchase finished goods to resell at a profit, as well as other goods and services to maintain their operations. Governments and other non-profit organizations purchase the goods and services necessary to fulfill their objectives.

3. A buying centre, or cross-functional team of decision makers, may be formed for a specific purchasing decision. Different members of the buying centre usually adopt one or more roles: initiator, user, gatekeeper, influencer, decider, or buyer.

Case Analysis

1. Ritvik Holdings is involved in manufacturing, which has a NAICS Sector code of 31-33.

2. Ritvik Holdings would be classified as a Producer, according to Figure 7.3 in Chapter 7.

3. The company's main clients are distributors and retailers; therefore, the company is involved in B2B Marketing.

4. Ritvik's European clients are concerned that the company's product packaging is not tailored to European requirements.

CHAPTER 8

Sharpening the Focus: Target Marketing Strategies

CHAPTER OVERVIEW

The purpose of this chapter was to understand the need for market segmentation and target marketing in today's business environment. Market segmentation and target marketing are important strategies in today's marketplace due to the splintering of mass society into diverse groups because of technological and cultural differences known as market fragmentation. Market segmentation means to divide a large market into a set of smaller markets that share important characteristics. In target marketing, marketers select one or more of these specific groups to serve.

In developing a segmentation strategy, marketers first examine consumer demand in relation to the product. If demand is homogenous, a mass market strategy where only one product is sold to the total market may be best. If demand is clustered or diffused, a segmented marketing strategy may be better. To choose one or more segments to target, marketers examine each segment and evaluate its potential for success as a target market.

Next, we considered the different dimensions used for segmenting consumer markets. Marketers frequently find it useful to segment consumer markets based on demographic characteristics including age, gender, family structure, social class, ethnicity, geographic location, or geodemography. Consumer markets may also be segmented based on consumer lifestyles and how consumers behave toward the product.

Categories similar to those in the consumer market are frequently used for segmenting industrial markets. Industrial demographics include industry and/or company size, North American Industry Classification System (NAICS) codes or geographic location. Industrial markets may also be segmented based on operating variables, purchasing approaches, and end-use applications.

After the different segments have been identified, the market potential of each segment is estimated, which influences the firm's selection of an overall marketing strategy. The firm may choose an undifferentiated, differentiated, concentrated, or custom strategy based on the company's characteristics and the nature of the market.

Finally, after the target market(s) and the overall strategy have been selected, marketers must determine how they wish their brand to be perceived by consumers relative to the competition. Marketers must continually monitor changes in the market that might indicate a need for repositioning of the product.

CHAPTER OBJECTIVES

1.   Understand the three steps involved in developing a target marketing strategy.

2.   Understand the need for market segmentation in today's business environment.

3.   Know the different dimensions marketers use to segment consumer markets.

4.   Understand the bases for segmentation in business-to-business markets.

5.   Explain how marketers evaluate and select potential market segments.

6.   Explain how marketers develop a targeting strategy.

7.   Understand how a firm develops and implements a positioning strategy.

CHAPTER OUTLINE

With reference to the textbook, please provide a brief description of each of the main elements listed in the Chapter Outline below. The page numbers will help guide you through the learning process.

I.   SELECTING AND ENTERING A MARKET
        Market Fragmentation _____ (p.202)
        Target Marketing Strategy _____ (p.203)

II.   SEGMENTATION _____ (p.203)
        Segmentation Variables _____ (p.203)
        A.   Dimensions For Segmenting Consumer Markets
                1.   Segmenting By Demographics
                        Age _____ (p.204)
                        Baby Boomers_____ (p.204)
                        Gender_____ (p.205)
                        Family Structure _____ (p.205)
                        Income and Social Class _____ (p.206)
                        Ethnicity _____ (p.206)
                        Geography_____ (p.207)
                        Geodemography _____ (p.209)
                2.   Segmenting By Psychographics _____ (p.210)
                        VALS™ (Values and Lifestyles) _____ (p.210)
                3.   Segmenting By Behaviour
                        Behavioural Segmentation _____ (p.211)
                        80/20 Rule_____ (p.211)
                        Usage Occasions _____ (p.211)

B. Dimensions For Segmenting Business Markets
   1. Organizational Demographics_____ *(p.212)*
   2. Company-Specific Characteristics _____ *(p.212)*
      Operating Variables _____ *(p.212)*

III. TARGETING
   Target Market _____ *(p.212)*
   A. Evaluate Market Segments
      1. Similar in needs, different from consumers in
         other segments_____ *(p.213)*
      2. Measurable _____ *(p.213)*
      3. Large enough to be profitable _____ *(p.213)*
      4. Reachable though marketing communications _____ *(p.214)*
      5. Segment's needs can be served_____ *(p.214)*

   B. Develop Segment Profiles
      Segment Profile_____ *(p.214)*
      Market Potential _____ *(p.214)*

   C. Choose A Targeting Strategy
      1. Undifferentiated Marketing
         Undifferentiated Targeting Strategy _____ *(p.216)*
      2. Differentiated Marketing
         Differentiated Targeting Strategy _____ *(p.216)*
      3. Concentrated Marketing
         Concentrated Targeting Strategy_____ *(p.216)*
      4. Custom Marketing: A "Segment of One"
         Custom Marketing Strategy _____ *(p.217)*
         Mass Customization _____ *(p.217)*

IV. POSITIONING _____ *(p.217)*
   A. Develop A Positioning Strategy _____ *(p.218)*
      1. Analyze Competitors' Positions _____ *(p.218)*
      2. Identify Competitive Advantage_____ *(p.218)*
      3. Finalize The Marketing Mix _____ *(p.218)*
      4. Evaluate The Target Market's Responses
         and Modify the Strategy _____ *(p.218)*
         Repositioning _____ *(p.218)*

   B. Positioning Dimensions_____ *(p.218)*
      1. Bringing A Product To Life:
         The Brand Personality_____ *(p.219)*
      2. Perceptual Mapping _____ *(p.219)*

KEY TERMS

Select the correct term for each definition and write it in the space provided.

Operating variables
Market potential
Target marketing strategy
Perceptual map
Geodemographics
Positioning
Differentiated targeting strategy
Market fragmentation

Segmentation
Brand personality
Concentrated targeting strategy
Segmentation variables
Custom marketing strategy
Usage occasions
VALS™ (Values and Lifestyles)

1. _____ Creation of many consumer groups die to a diversity of distinct needs and wants in modern society. *(p.202)*

2. _____ Dividing the total market into different segments based on customer characteristics, selecting one or more segments, and developing products to meet the needs of those specific segments. *(p.202)*

3. _____ A process of dividing a larger customer market into smaller pieces, based on one or more meaningful, shared characteristics. *(p.203)*

4. _____ An indicator that is used in one type of market segmentation based on when consumers use a product most. *(p.211)*

5. _____ The production technology used, the business customer's degree of technical, financial, or operations expertise, and whether or not the prospect is a current user or nonuser of the product. *(p.212)*

6. _____ Bases for dividing the total market into fairly homogenous groups, each with different needs and preferences. *(p.203)*

7. _____ Segmentation technique that combines geography with demographics. *(p.206)*

Marketing: Real People, Real Decisions

8. _____*vals*_____   A psychographic system that divides people into eight segments. *(p.210)*

9. _____MP_____   The maximum demand expected among consumers in a potential market segment for a good or service. *(p.214)*

10. _____D+s_____   A marketing strategy in which a firm develops one or more products for each of several distinct customer groups. *(p.216)*

11. _____C+s_____   A marketing strategy in which a firm focuses its efforts on offering one or more products to a single segment. *(p.216)*

12. _____CMs_____   Approach that tailors specific products and the messages about them to individual customers. *(p.217)*

13. _____P_____   A marketing strategy aimed at influencing how a particular market segment perceives a product or service in comparison to the competition. *(p.217)*

14. _____BP_____   A distinctive image that captures a product or service's character and benefits. *(p.219)*

15. _____PM_____   A picture of where products or brands are "located" in consumers' minds. *(p.219)*

MULTIPLE CHOICE

Identify the most correct answer.

1. _____occurs when people's diverse interests and backgrounds have divided them into different groups with distinct needs and wants. *(p.202)*
   a.   broadcasting.
   b.   mass marketing.
   c.   segmenting.
   d.   market fragmentation.

abadc dabdc
abdca.

2.   A positioning strategy: *(p.217)*
      a.   divides the overall market into market segments.
      b.   involves the creation of a marketing strategy aimed at influencing how a particular market segment perceives a product or service in comparison to the competition.
      c.   provides a comparative advantage over rival offerings in the minds of the segment members.
      d.   all of the above.

3.   The segment of Canadians born between 1947 and 1966 is called: *(p.204)*
      a.   baby boomers.
      b.   millennium busters.
      c.   baby busters.
      d.   baby boom echo.

4.   For a demand segment to be usable, it should satisfy the following criterion/criteria: *(p.213)*
      a.   the segment can be measured and understood.
      b.   the segment is large enough to be profitable, now and in the future.
      c.   the marketer can adequately serve the needs of the segment.
      d.   all of the above.

5.   Characteristics of a population that are easy to identify and for which information is easily obtained are called: *(p.204)*
      a.   geographics.
      b.   geneologies.
      c.   demographics.
      d.   generations.

6.   The following factor(s) make the Aboriginal segment attractive to marketers: *(p.206)*
      a.   half of all Aboriginals in Canada are under the age of thirty.
      b.   aboriginal consumer income is rising faster than that of other Canadians.
      c.   there are over one million Aboriginals in Canada.
      d.   all of the above.

7.   A way to segment consumer markets based on how they act toward, feel about, or use a good or service is called: *(p.211)*
      a.   behavioural segmentation.
      b.   geodemography.
      c.   lifestyle segmentation.
      d.   VALS™.

8.   Behavioural segmentation means: *(p.211)*
      a.   consumers make a conscious decision to keep buying the same brand.
      b.   dividing consumers into segments on the basis of how they act toward, feel about, or use a product or service.
      c.   consumers make a purchase out of habit.
      d.   consumers will vary in terms of their current interest in purchasing a product.

9. A description of the "typical" customer in a market segment. *(p.214)*
    a.   segment fragment.
    b.   fragment target.
    c.   custom profile.
    d.   segment profile.

10. A marketing strategy that attempts to appeal to a broad spectrum of people is known as a(n): *(p.216)*
    a.   differentiated marketing strategy.
    b.   counter segmentation strategy.
    c.   undifferentiated marketing strategy.
    d.   maximized marketing strategy.

11. A target market is a: *(p.212)*
    a.   group or groups selected by a firm to be turned into customers as a result of segmentation and targeting.
    b.   market in which a firm focuses its efforts on offering one or more products to several segments.
    c.   market in which a firm develops a separate marketing mix for each customer.
    d.   all of the above.

12. A marketing strategy in which a firm modifies a basic good or service to meet the needs of an individual customer is called: *(p.217)*
    a.   differentiated marketing strategy.
    b.   mass customization.
    c.   unique segmentation.
    d.   modified marketing strategy.

13. The following guideline(s) often apply to effective targeting strategies: *(p.216)*
    a.   An undifferentiated strategy is often appropriate for products that people perceive as basically homogenous.
    b.   A concentrated or custom strategy is often useful for smaller firms that do not have the resources or the desire to be all things to all people.
    c.   The choice of a strategy tends to change as the product moves through the life cycle.
    d.   All of the above.

14. A marketing rule of thumb that 20 percent of purchasers account for 80 percent of a product's sales is called the: *(p.211)*
    a.   20/80 rule.
    b.   market percentage rule.
    c.   80/20 rule.
    d.   target market rule.

15. Redoing a product's position to respond to marketplace change is called: *(p.218)*
    a. repositioning.
    b. image advantage strategy.
    c. adjustment segmentation.
    d. competitive identification.

CHAPTER IN REVIEW—WRITING TO LEARN

1. Describe market segmentation and target marketing.

_____

_____

_____

_____

2. Identify the bases for segmentation in business markets.

_____

_____

_____

_____

3. Explain how potential market segments are evaluated and selected.

_____

_____

_____

_____

CASE ANALYSIS

Real People, Real Decisions: Candace Fochuk-Barey, Ford Motor Company of Canada

Reread the three sections comprising the Ford Motor Company vignette in Chapter 8 and answer the following questions:

1. What is one of Ford's priority target markets?

2. What did Ford's research reveal about the auto buying behaviour of women?

3. According to Ford's research, what are women looking for in an automobile?

4. Which marketing activities did Ford undertake specifically to serve the needs of women?

SCENARIO

You are the Director of Marketing for a company that is launching a new brand of cereal. You really want your cereal to stand out—in advertising and on grocer's shelves. You are hoping to target a segment of the market that will allow you to position your cereal in a way that is "different and better" than competitors' offerings, and at the same time, produce a reasonable profit for your company.

Before proceeding with decisions about the marketing mix (i.e. product, price, promotion, place), you decide to "sharpen your focus", by undertaking the following tasks:

1. Visit your nearest supermarket and bring a notepad. Write down the various cereal brands and their prices. Note the packaging and promotion (e.g., giveaways, etc.), and try to determine whom it is trying to attract. Notice which shelf the cereal is displayed on (the highest? The lowest?) and try to figure out what that means.
2. Using the information you obtained at the supermarket, develop a "perceptual map" of the cereal market (see page 219-220 in your text), using the following dimensions: price and quality.
3. Using the information you obtained at the supermarket, develop a "perceptual map" of the cereal market (see page 219-220 in your text), using the following dimensions: age and income (of group targeted).
4. Now, examine your perceptual maps. Are there any blank areas where your cereal could be positioned and if so, where (i.e., which specific dimensions) are they on the maps? What is the resulting positioning? Is it a positioning that your company could profitably pursue? Why or why not?

ANSWERS

Chapter Outline

I.   SELECTING AND ENTERING A MARKET

Market Fragmentation—Creation of many consumer groups due to a diversity of distinct needs and wants in modern society.

Target Marketing Strategy—Base for dividing the total market into different segments based on customer characteristics, selecting one or more segments, and developing products to meet the needs of those specific segments.

II.   SEGMENTATION—The process of dividing a larger market into smaller pieces based on one or more meaningful, shared characteristics.

Segmentation Variables—Divide the total market into fairly homogeneous groups, each with different needs and preferences.

A.   Dimensions For Segmenting Consumer Markets

1.   Segmenting By Demographics

Age—Consumers of different age groups have very different needs and wants.

Baby Boomers—Segment of people born between 1947 and 1966.

Baby Bust—Group of consumers born between 1967 and 1979.

Baby Boom Echo—Group of consumers born between 1980 and 1995.

Millennium Busters: Group of consumers born between 1996 and 2010.

Gender—Many products appeal to either men or women, thus segmenting the market by sex.

Family Structure—Family needs and expenditures change over time, as well as the stage of the family life cycle.

Income and Social Class—The distribution of wealth is of great interest to marketers because it determines which groups have the greatest buying power.

Ethnicity—Can have a strong impact on consumers' preferences for goods and services.

Geography—People's preferences often depend on which region of the country they live in.

Geodemography—Technique used by marketers to segment markets that combines geography with demographics.

2.   Segmenting By Psychographics—Segmenting the market in terms of shared attitudes, interests, and opinions.

VALS™ (Values and Lifestyles)—Psychographic system that divides people into eight segments.

3.   Segmenting By Behaviour

Behavioural Segmentation—Technique that divides consumers into segments on the basis of how they act toward, feel about, or use a product or service.

80/20 Rule—A marketing rule of thumb that 20 percent of purchasers account for 80 percent of a product's sales.

Usage Occasions—Indicator used in one type of market segmentation based on when consumers use a product most.

B.   Dimensions For Segmenting Business Markets

1.   Organizational Demographics—Many marketers use the North American Industry Classification System (NAICS) to learn more about a particular industry.

2.   Company-Specific Characteristics—Each firm has certain characteristics that influence the types of products and services it needs.

3.   Operating Variables—The production technology used, the business customer's degree of technical, financial, or operations expertise, and whether or not the prospect is a current user or nonuser of the product.

III.   TARGETING
       Target Markets—Group or groups selected by a firm to be turned into customers, as a result of segmentation and targeting.
       A.   Evaluate Market Segments
            1.   Are members of the segment similar to each other in their product needs and wants and at the same time, different from consumers in other segments?
            2.   Can marketers measure the segment?
            3.   Is the segment large enough to be profitable now and in the future?
            4.   Can marketing communications reach the segment?
            5.   Can the marketer adequately serve the needs of the segment?

       B.   Develop Segment Profiles
            Segment Profile—A description of the "typical" customer in a segment.
            Market Potential—The maximum demand expected among consumers in a segment for a product or service.

       C.   Choose A Targeting Strategy
            1.   Undifferentiated Marketing
                 Undifferentiated Targeting Strategy—Technique of attempting to appeal to a broad spectrum of people.
            2.   Differentiated Marketing
                 Differentiated Targeting Strategy—Developing one or more products for each of several distinct customer group sand making sure these offerings are kept separate in the marketplace.
            3.   Concentrated Marketing
                 Concentrated Targeting Strategy—Focusing a firm's efforts on offering one or more products to a single segment.
            4.   Custom Marketing: A "Segment Of One"
                 Custom Marketing Strategy—Approach that tailors specific products and the messages about them to individual customers.
                 Mass Customization—Approach that modifies a basic product or service to meet the needs of an individual.

IV.   POSITIONING—Developing a marketing strategy aimed at influencing how a particular market segment perceives a product or service in comparison to the competition.
       A.   Developing A Positioning Strategy—The success of a target marketing strategy hinges on marketers' abilities to identify and select an appropriate market segment.
            1.   Analyze Competitors' Positions—What competitors are out there, and how are they perceived by the target market?
            2.   Identify Competitive Advantage—To provide a reason why consumers will perceive the product as better than the competition.
            3.   Finalize The Marketing Mix—The elements of the marketing mix must match the selected segment.
            4.   Evaluate The Target Market's Responses And Modify The Strategy—The firm may find that it needs to change which segments it targets, and the needs of people may change as well.
                 Repositioning—Redoing a product's position to respond to marketplace changes.

       B.   Positioning Dimensions—Lifestyle image, Price leadership, Attributes, Product class, Competitors, Occasions, Users, and Quality.
            1.   Bringing A Product To Life: The Brand Personality—A distinctive image that captures a product or service's character and benefits.
            2.   Perceptual Mapping—A picture of where products or brands are "located" in consumers' minds.

Key Terms

1. Market fragmentation
2. Target marketing strategy
3. Segmentation
4. Usage occasions
5. Operating variables
6. Segmentation variables
7. Geodemography
8. VALS™ (Values and Lifestyles)
9. Market potential
10. Differentiated targeting strategy
11. Concentrated targeting strategy
12. Custom marketing strategy
13. Positioning
14. Brand personality
15. Perceptual map

Multiple Choice

1. d
2. b
3. a
4. d
5. c
6. d
7. a
8. b
9. d
10. c
11. a
12. b
13. d
14. c
15. a

Chapter in Review—Writing to Learn

1. Market segmentation means to divide a large market into a set of smaller markets that share important characteristics. In target marketing, marketers select one or more of these specific groups to serve. The development of a clear and positive image to communicate to members of the target market groups is called positioning.

2. Categories similar to those in the consumer market are frequently used for segmenting business markets. Organizational demographics include industry and/or company size, North America Industry Classification System (NAICS) codes or geographic location. Business markets may also be segmented based on operating variables, purchasing approaches, and end use applications.

3. After the different segments have been identified, the market potential of each segment is estimated. The relative attractiveness of segments is also influenced by the firm's selection of an overall marketing strategy. The firm may choose an undifferentiated, differentiated, concentrated or custom marketing strategy based on the company's characteristics and the nature of the market.

Case Analysis

1. One of Ford's priority target markets is women, 24-54 years of age.

2. Ford's research on women's automobile buying behaviour found that women take more time to search for information before making a purchase, and like to purchase from a company that they feel cares about their customers and the community.

3. Women car buyers are looking for reliability, durability, good value, easy handling, and a good warranty.

4. To address the needs of the women's market, Ford developed a special course for its dealers, recruited more female salespeople, sponsored Run for the Cure (a fundraising event for breast cancer research), and ran seminars for women on topics such as car maintenance and car seat safety.

CHAPTER 9

Creating the Product

CHAPTER OVERVIEW

We began this chapter by defining the three dimensions of a product. The core product is the basic product category benefits and customized benefit(s) the product provides. The actual product is the physical good or delivered service, including the packaging and brand name. The augmented product includes both the actual product and any supplementary services such as warranty, credit, delivery, installation, etc.

Next, we described the ways in which products are classified. Consumer products can be classified according to how long they last. Durable goods provide benefits for months or years. Nondurable goods are used up quickly or are useful for only a short time. Consumer products are also classified by how they are purchased. This classification approach includes convenience products, shopping products, specialty products, and unsought products. Business products are classified according to how they are used. New products are anything consumers perceive to be new and may be classified as continuous innovations, dynamically continuous innovations or discontinuous innovations.

We then discussed the process of product adoption and the diffusion process. Product adoption describes how an individual begins to use a new product. The diffusion process describes how a new product spreads through a population. The stages in the adoption process are awareness, interest, evaluation, trial, adoption, and confirmation. Individuals may be classified according to their readiness to adopt new products: innovators, early adopters, early majority, late majority, and laggards. Five product characteristics that have an important effect on how quickly (or whether) a new product will be adopted by consumers are relative advantage, compatibility, product complexity, trialability, and product observability.

CHAPTER OBJECTIVES

1.   Explain the layers of a product.

2.   Describe the classifications of products.

3.   Explain the importance of new products.

4.   Describe how firms develop new products.

5.   Explain the process of product adoption and the diffusion of innovations.

CHAPTER OUTLINE

With reference to the textbook, please provide a brief description of each of the main elements listed in the Chapter Outline below. The page numbers will help guide you through the learning process.

I.   BUILD A BETTER MOUSETRAP
        Goks _____ *(p.234)*
        A.   Layers Of The Product Concept
                1.   The Core Product _____ *(p.236)*
                2.   The Actual Product _____ *(p.237)*
                3.   The Augmented Product _____ *(p.237)*

II.   CLASSIFYING PRODUCTS
        A.   Consumer Product Classes Defined By How Long
                A Product Lasts
                Durable Goods _____ *(p.237)*
                Nondurable Goods _____ *(p.237)*
        B.   Consumer Product Classes Defined By How Consumers
                Buy The Product
                Convenience Product _____ *(p.239)*
                Shopping Product _____ *(p.239)*
                Specialty Product _____ *(p.240)*
        C.   Business-to-Business Products
                Equipment _____ *(p.241)*
                Maintenance, Repair, and Operating (MRO) Products _____ *(p.241)*
                Raw Materials _____ *(p.241)*
                Processed Materials _____ *(p.241)*
                Specialized Services _____ *(p.241)*
                Component Parts _____ *(p.241)*

III.   IT'S NEW AND IMPROVED! UNDERSTANDING INNOVATIONS
        Innovations _____ *(p.241)*
        A.   The Importance of Understanding Innovations _____ *(p.242)*
        B.   Types of Innovations _____ *(p.242)*
                1.   Continuous Innovation _____ *(p.243)*
                        Knock-off _____ *(p.243)*
                2.   Dynamically Continuous Innovation _____ *(p.243)*
                3.   Discontinuous Innovation _____ *(p.244)*

IV.   DEVELOPING NEW PRODUCTS _____ (p.245)
    A.   The Visionary Phase _____ (p.245)
    B.   Planning and Development _____ (p.247)
         Commercial Development_____ (p.247)
         Technical Development_____ (p.248)
    C.   Testing and Improving the Product
         Test Marketing_____ (p.248)

V.   ADOPTION AND DIFFUSION PROCESSES
    Product Adoption_____ (p.249)
    Diffusion _____ (p.249)
    A.   Stages in a Customer's Adoption of a New Product _____ (p.246)
         1.   Awareness _____ (p.249)
         2.   Interest_____ (p.249)
         3.   Evaluation _____ (p.249)
         4.   Trial _____ (p.250)
         5.   Adoption _____ (p.250)
         6.   Confirmation _____ (p.251)
    B.   The Diffusion Of Innovations _____ (p.251)
         1.   Adopter Categories
         Innovators _____ (p.251)
         Early Adopters _____ (p.251)
         Early Majority_____ (p.252)
         Late Majority_____ (p.252)
         Laggards _____ (p.253)
         2.   Product Factors Affecting the Rate of Adoption
         Relative Advantage _____ (p.253)
         Compatibility_____ (p.254)
         Complexity _____ (p.254)
         Trialability_____ (p.254)
         Observability_____ (p.254)
    C.   Organizational Differences Affect Adoption_____ (p.254)

KEY TERMS

Select the correct term for each definition and write it in the space provided.

Specialty product	Laggards
Discontinuous innovation	Innovation
Goods	Raw materials
Innovators	Convenience product
Durable goods	Diffusion
Continuous innovation	Component parts
Processed materials	Early majority
Equipment	

1. _____   Tangible products we can see, touch, smell and/or taste. *(p.234)*

2. _____   Manufactured goods or subassemblies of finished items that organizations need to complete their own products. *(p.241)*

3. _____   Consumer products that provide benefits over a period of time such as cars, furniture, and appliances. *(p.237)*

4. _____   A consumer good or service which is usually low priced, widely available, and purchased frequently, with a minimum of comparison and effort. *(p.239)*

5. _____   A good or service that has unique characteristics, is very important to the buyer, and for which the buyer will devote significant effort to acquire. *(p.240)*

6. _____   A product that consumers perceive to be new and different from existing products. *(p.241)*

7. _____   A modification of an existing product used to set one brand apart from its competitors. *(p.243)*

8. _____   A totally new product that creates major changes in the way we live. *(p.244)*

9. _____   The process by which the use of an innovation spreads throughout a population. *(p.249)*

10. _____   The first segment (roughly 2.5%) of a population to adopt a product. *(p.251)*

11. _____   The approximately 34% of the population whose adoption of a new product signals a general acceptance of the innovation. *(p.252)*

12. _____   The roughly 16% of consumers who are the last to adopt an innovation. *(p.253)*

13. _____ Expensive goods an organization uses in its daily operations that last for a long time. *(p.241)*

14. _____ Products created when firms transform raw materials from their original state. *(p.241)*

15. _____ Products of the fishing, lumber, agricultural, and mining industries that organizational customers purchase to use in their finished products. *(p.241)*

MULTIPLE CHOICE

Identify the most correct answer.

1. The outcome sought by a customer that motivates buying behaviour; the value the customer receives from owning, using, or experiencing a product is known as: *(p.236)*
   a. the product promotion.
   b. product augmentation.
   c. the benefit of a product.
   d. the product desirability.

2. Consumer products that provide benefits for only a short time because they are consumed (such as food) or are no longer useful (such as newspapers) are: *(p.237)*
   a. convenience products.
   b. durable goods.
   c. disposable products.
   d. nondurable goods.

3. A shopping product is: *(p.239)*
   a. a good or service for which consumers will spend considerable time and effort gathering information and comparing a number of different alternatives before making a purchase.
   b. a consumer good or service which is usually low-priced, widely available, and purchased frequently, with a minimum of comparison and effort.
   c. a good or service that has unique characteristics, is very important to the buyer, and for which the buyer will devote significant effort to acquire.
   d. a product that is only needed and purchased when necessary.

4.   A good or service for a consumer has little awareness or interest until the product or a need for the product is brought to his/her attention is called a(n): *(p.240)*
     a.   convenience product.
     b.   unsought product.
     c.   innovation.
     d.   specialty product.

5.   A knock-off is: *(p.243)*
     a.   a new product that has not been accepted by consumers.
     b.   a reduction in the initial pricing of a product.
     c.   a new product that copies with slight modification the design of an original product.
     d.   a new type of insect spray.

6.   A continuous innovation: *(p.243)*
     a.   is a more pronounced change in an existing product.
     b.   will have a modest impact on the way people do things, creating some behavioural changes.
     c.   includes such products as a self-focusing 35mm cameras and a 900 MHz cordless telephone.
     d.   all of the above.

7.   The process by which a consumer or business customer begins to use a good, service, or an idea is known as: *(p.249)*
     a.   product adoption.
     b.   product diffusion.
     c.   product adaptation.
     d.   product availability.

8.   The first necessary step in the product adoption process is: *(p.249)*
     a.   interest.
     b.   awareness of the innovation.
     c.   evaluation.
     d.   trial.

9.   The approximately 13.5% of adopters who adopt an innovation very early in the diffusion process but after the innovators are: *(p.251)*
     a.   early majority.
     b.   late innovators.
     c.   first-time buyers.
     d.   early adopters.

10.   The roughly 34% of adopters who are willing to try new products only when there is little or no risk associated with the purchase, when the purchase becomes an economic necessity or when there is social pressure to purchase are: *(p.252)*

    a.   laggards.

    b.   early majority.

    c.   late majority.

    d.   pressure adopters.

11.   The degree to which a new product is perceived to provide benefits superior to those provided by the product it replaces is called: *(p.253)*

    a.   comparative advantage.

    b.   relative advantage.

    c.   competitive advantage.

    d.   absolute advantage.

12.   The extent to which a new product is consistent with existing cultural values, customers, and practices is: *(p.254)*

    a.   compatibility.

    b.   adaptability.

    c.   complexity.

    d.   convenience.

13.   Observability refers to: *(p.254)*

    a.   the degree to which individuals find a new product or its use difficult to understand.

    b.   the ease of sampling a new product and its benefits.

    c.   how visible a new product and its benefits are to others who might adopt the innovation.

    d.   how the firm has marketed its product to the target market.

14.   The degree to which consumers find a new product or its use difficult to understand refers to a product's: *(p.254)*

    a.   trialability.

    b.   complexity.

    c.   compatibility.

    d.   observability.

15.   The ease of sampling a new product and its benefits is: *(p.254)*

    a.   observability.

    b.   complexity.

    c.   compatibility.

    d.   trialability.

CHAPTER IN REVIEW—WRITING TO LEARN

1.   Explain the three dimensions of a product.

_____

_____

_____

_____

2.   Describe the product classifications of consumer products.

_____

_____

_____

_____

3.   What are the five product characteristics that have an important effect on how quickly (or whether) a new product will be adopted by consumers?

_____

_____

_____

CASE ANALYSIS

Real People, Real Decisions: Marshall Myles, Roots

1.   Since its first product, the negative-heel shoe, Roots has significantly broadened its product line. Which other products has the company introduced?

2.   Which major new product initiative did Roots undertake in the early 1980s?

3.   The majority of Roots products fall into which consumer product class?

4.   If Roots decided to launch Roots Kids stores, what *type* of innovation would the company be undertaking—and why?

SCENARIO

You are a product manager at a major financial institution. You are responsible for the marketing of chequing accounts. You are considering the introduction of a new chequing account that would have a new pricing structure, which would reflect the number of transactions made and where they were made (teller, Automated Banking Machine (ABM), phone or Internet. As you embark on the new product development process, you decide that it is important to revisit the fundamentals first, so you ask yourself the following questions:

1.   Is a chequing account a durable or nondurable good—and what impact will that have on what potential customers consider before choosing my product?

2.   Is a chequing account a convenience product, a shopping product, a specialty product or an unsought product—and what impact will this have on the process customers go through to choose my product?

3.   Will customers consider my new account to be a continuous innovation, a knock-off, a dynamically continuous innovation, or a discontinuous innovation—and what impact will this have on whether customers choose to move to my new account?

4.   Which steps should I take to move my customers quickly through the adoption process, from awareness to confirmation?

ANSWERS

Chapter Outline

I.   BUILD A BETTER MOUSETRAP
Goods—Tangible products we can see, touch, smell, hear, or taste.
  A.   Layers Of The Product Concept
    1.   The Core Product—Consists of all the benefits the product will provide for consumers or business customers.
    2.   The Actual Product—Is the physical good or the delivered service that supplied the desired benefit.
    3.   The Augmented Product—The actual product plus other supporting features such as a warranty, credit, delivery, installation, and repair service after the sale.

II.   CLASSIFYING PRODUCTS
  A.   Consumer Product Classes Defined By How Long A Product Lasts.
Durable Goods—Consumer products that provide benefits over a period of time such as cars, furniture, and appliances.
Non-durable Goods—Consumer products that provide benefits for a short time because they are consumed (such as food) or are no longer useful (such as newspapers).

  B.   Consumer Product Classes Defined By How Consumers Buy the Product
Convenience Product—A consumer good or service that is usually low priced, widely available, and purchased frequently, with a minimum of comparison and effort.
Shopping Product—A good or service for which consumers will spend considerable time and effort gathering information and comparing alternatives before making a purchase.
Specialty Product—A good or service that has unique characteristics, is important to the buyer, and for which the buyer will devote significant effort to acquire.

  C.   Business-to-Business Products
Equipment—Expensive goods an organization uses in its daily operations that last for a long time.
Maintenance, Repair, and Operating (MRO) Products—Goods that a business customer consumes in a relatively short time.
Raw Materials—Products of the fishing, lumber, agricultural, and mining industries that organizational customers purchase to use in their finished products.
Processed Materials—Products created when firms transform raw materials from their original state.
Specialized Services—Services purchased from outside suppliers that are essential to the operation of an organization but are not part of the production of a product.
Component Parts—Manufactured goods or subassemblies of finished items that organizations need to complete their own products.

III. IT'S NEW AND IMPROVED! UNDERSTANDING INNOVATIONS
Innovation—A product that consumers perceive to be new and different from existing products.
  A.   The Importance of Understanding Innovations—Technology is advancing at a dizzying pace. In addition, the high cost of developing new products and the even higher cost of new products that fail can be a serious concern.

B.   Types of Innovations.
Innovations—Differ in their degree of newness, and this helps to determine how quickly the products will be adopted by many members of a target market.
1.   Continuous Innovation—A modification of an existing product that sets one brand apart from its competitors.
Knock-off—A new product that copies with slight modification the design of an original product.
2.   Dynamically Continuous Innovation—A change in an existing product that requires a moderate amount of learning or behaviour change.
3.   Discontinuous Innovation—A totally new product that creates major changes in the way we live.

IV.   DEVELOPING NEW PRODUCTS—New-product development occurs in three phases.
A.   The Visionary Phase—In the visionary phase of product development, marketers generate new-product ideas, screen new-product concepts, and complete a business analysis.

B.   Planning And Development—If it survives the scrutiny of a business analysis, a new-product concept then undergoes commercial and technical development.
Commercial Development—Putting together a marketing plan that builds on the initial projections made during product screening and business analysis.
Technical Development—A firm's engineers work with marketers to refine the design and production process.

C.   Testing And Improving The Product
Test Marketing—Testing the complete plan in a small geographic area that is similar to the larger market the firm hopes to enter.

V.   ADOPTION AND DIFFUSION PROCESSES
Product Adoption—The process by which a consumer or business customers begins to buy and use a new good, service, or an idea.
Diffusion—The process by which the use of a product spreads throughout a population.
A.   Stages in a Customer's Adoption of a New Product—Individuals and organizations pass through six stages in the adoption process.
1.   Awareness—Learning that the innovation exists is the first step in the adoption process.
2.   Interest—A prospective adopter begins to see how a new product might satisfy an existing or newly realized need.
3.   Evaluation—In the evaluation stage, a prospect weighs the costs and benefits of a new product.
4.   Trial—The potential adopters will actually experience or use the product for the first time.
5.   Adoption—A prospect chooses a product.
6.   Confirmation—Favourable experiences contribute to new customers becoming loyal adopters.

B.   The Diffusion Of Innovations—Describes how the use of a product spreads throughout a population.
1.   Adopter Categories
Innovators—The first segment (roughly 2.5 percent) of a population to adopt a new product.
Early Adopters—Those who adopt an innovation early in the diffusion process but after the innovators.
Early Majority—Those whose adoption of a new product signals a general acceptance of the innovation.
Late Majority—The adopters who are willing to try new products only when there is little or no risk associated with the purchase, when the purchase becomes an economic necessity or when there is social pressure to purchase.
Laggards—The last consumers to adopt an innovation.

2. Product Factors Affecting the Rate of Adoption

Relative Advantage—The degree to which a consumer perceives that a new product provides superior benefits.

Compatibility—The extent to which a new product is consistent with existing cultural values, customs, and practices.

Complexity—The degree to which consumers find a new product or its use difficult to understand.

Trialability—The ease of sampling a new product and its benefits.

Observability—How visible a new product and its benefits are to others who might adopt it.

C. Organizational Differences Affect Adoption—Businesses and other organizations are not alike in their willingness to buy and use new industrial products.

Key Terms

1. Goods
2. Component parts
3. Durable goods
4. Convenience product
5. Specialty product
6. Innovation
7. Continuous innovation
8. Discontinuous innovation
9. Diffusion
10. Innovators
11. Early majority
12. Laggards
13. Equipment
14. Processed materials
15. Raw materials

Multiple Choice

1. c
2. d
3. a
4. b
5. c
6. d
7. a
8. b
9. d
10. c
11. b
12. a
13. c
14. b
15. d

Chapter in Review—Writing to Learn

1. A product may be a tangible physical good or an intangible service or idea. The core product is the basic product category benefits and customized benefit(s) the product provides. The actual product is the physical good or delivered service including the packaging and brand name. The augmented product includes both the actual product and any supplementary services such as warranty, credit, delivery, installation, etc.

2. *Convenience* products are purchased frequently with little effort. *Shopping* products are bought only after customers carefully gather information and compare different brands on their attributes and/or price. *Specialty* products have unique characteristics and are important to the buyer. Customers have little interest in *unsought* products until a need arises.

3. Five product characteristics that have an important effect on how quickly (or whether) a new product will be adopted by consumers are 1) *relative advantage*, a product ability to provide important benefits; 2) *compatibility* with a consumer's normal way of doing things; 3) product *complexity*, 4) *trialability* or the ability to sample or try out a new product; and 5) product *observability*, the likelihood that other people will readily observe the new product and its benefits.

Case Analysis

1.   Since its first product, Roots has broadened its product line considerably, and now markets everything from shoes and home furnishings to the clothing worn by the Canadian and U.S. Olympic teams during the 2002 Winter Olympics held in Salt Lake City, Utah.

2.   In the early 1980s, Roots introduced a line of children's clothing.

3.   Most Roots products would be classified as shopping products, because, prior to buying them, most consumers would spend considerable time gathering information and comparing alternatives.

4.   Roots Kids stores are an example of a dynamically continuous innovation, because customers will be required to change their behaviour, i.e., they used to buy Roots kids clothing at Roots stores; now they will have to shop at a different store.

CHAPTER 10

Managing the Product

CHAPTER OVERVIEW

In this chapter, we first learned about some of the different product strategies a firm may choose. Product objectives support broader marketing objectives of a firm and ideally, focus on customer needs. Objectives for individual products may be related to introducing the product, rejuvenating an existing product, or harvesting a declining product. Other strategies focus on entire product lines, different product items that satisfy the same customer need. Marketers may determine that the best strategy is to extend the product line with an upward stretch, a downward stretch, or a two-way stretch. In other cases, objectives relate to a firm's product mix or the product quality.

One way that firms manage existing products is with a brand management structure where individual brand managers supervise all the marketing activities for a single brand. New products are sometimes both created and managed by entrepreneurs; however, large firms often give new product responsibilities to new product managers who develop marketing plans for the many different new products the firm develops. In other cases, new products are managed by venture teams. Managing an existing product requires understanding its stage in the product life cycle—whether it is the introductory, growth, maturity, or decline stage.

Packaging and labelling play an important role in the development of effective product strategies. Package design communicates a product's identity, benefits, and other important product information. Package labelling in Canada is controlled by a number of federal laws aimed at making package labels more helpful to consumers.

Finally, we reviewed how branding creates product identity and the different types of branding strategies. A brand is a name, logo, trade character or some other recognizable element that is used to identify or position a product or to convey product attributes. Brands are important because they help in developing and maintaining customer loyalty and help to create value or brand equity. Different categories of brands include brand extensions, family brands, national or manufacturer brands, and private label or store brands. Types of branding strategies include licensing agreements and co-branding strategies.

CHAPTER OBJECTIVES

1.   Explain the different product objectives and strategies a firm may choose.

2.   Explain how firms manage products throughout the product life cycle.

3.   Discuss how branding creates product identity and describe different types of branding strategies.

4.   Explain the roles packaging and labelling play in developing effective product strategies.

5.   Describe how organizations are structured for new and existing product management.

CHAPTER OUTLINE

With reference to the textbook, please provide a brief description of each of the main elements listed in the Chapter Outline below. The page numbers will help guide you through the learning process.

I.   CREATING AND NURTURING QUALITY PRODUCTS _____ *(p.262)*

II.   USING PRODUCT OBJECTIVES TO DECIDE ON A
        PRODUCT STRATEGY_____ *(p.262)*
        A.   Objectives And Strategies For Individual Products_____ *(p.263)*
        B.   Objectives And Strategies For Multiple Products
                1.   Product Line Strategies _____ *(p.264)*
                        Full-Line Strategy _____ *(p.264)*
                        Limited-Line Strategy _____ *(p.265)*
                        Stretching The Firm's Product Line _____ *(p.265)*
                        Cannibalization _____ *(p.266)*
                        Product Mix_____ *(p.266)*
        C.   Quality As A Product Objective _____ *(p.266)*

III.   MARKETING THROUGHOUT THE PRODUCT LIFE CYCLE __ *(p.267)*
        A.   The Introduction Stag _____ *(p.267)*
        B.   The Growth Stage _____ *(p.267)*
        C.   The Maturity Stage _____ *(p.269)*
        D.   The Decline Stage _____ *(p.269)*

IV.   CREATING PRODUCT IDENTITY: BRANDING DECISIONS
        A.   What's In A Name (Or A Symbol)?
                Brand _____ *(p.270)*
                1.   Choosing A Brand Name, Mark, Or Character_____ *(p.271)*
                2.   Trademarks _____ *(p.272)*
        B.   The Importance Of Branding
                Brand Equity _____ *(p.272)*
                Brand Extension _____ *(p.273)*
        C.   Branding Strategies
                1.   Individual Brands Versus Family Brands
                        Individual Brand Strategy _____ *(p.273)*
                        Family Brand_____ *(p.273)*
                2.   National and Store Brands
                        National or Manufacturer Brands _____ *(p.274)*
                        Store or Private-Label Brands_____ *(p.274)*
                3.   Licensing_____ *(p.275)*
                4.   Co-Branding _____ *(p.275)*

V.   CREATING PRODUCT IDENTITY: PACKAGING AND LABELLING DECISIONS
        A.   Packaging Functions
                Package _____ *(p.275)*
        B.   Designing Effective Packaging _____ *(p.277)*
        C.   Labelling Regulations _____ *(p.277)*

VI.   ORGANIZING FOR EFFECTIVE PRODUCT MANAGEMENT
        A.   Management Of Existing Products _____ *(p.278)*
                1.   Brand Manager _____ *(p.278)*
                2.   Product Category Manager _____ *(p.278)*
                3.   Market Manager _____ *(p.278)*
        B.   Organizing For New-Product Development _____ *(p.278)*
                Venture Teams_____ *(p.279)*

KEY TERMS

Select the correct term for each definition and write it in the space provided.

Venture teams   Brand equity
Trademark   Product line
Brand Manager   Brand extensions
Green Packaging   Market manager
Product life cycle   Growth stage
Cannibalization   Licensing
National or manufacturer brands   Product mix
Brand

1. _____ A firm's total product offering designed to satisfy a single need or desire of target customers. *(p.264)*

2. _____ The loss of sales of an existing product when a new item in a product line or product family is introduced. *(p.266)*

3. _____ The total set of all products a firm offers for sale by a firm. *(p.266)*

4. _____ A manager who is responsible for developing and implementing the marketing plan for a single brand. *(p.278)*

5. _____ A manager who is responsible for developing and implementing the marketing plans for products sold to a specific customer group. *(p.278)*

6. _____ Groups of people within an organization who work together focusing exclusively on the development of a new product. *(p.279)*

7. _____ The concept that explains how products go through four distinct stages from birth to death: introduction, growth, maturity, and decline. *(p.267)*

8. _____ The second stage in the product life cycle, during which the product is accepted and sales rapidly increase. *(p.269)*

9. _____ A name, a term, a symbol, or any other unique element of a product, which identifies one firm's product(s) and sets them apart from the competition. *(p.271)*

10. _____ The legal name for a brand name, brand mark, or trade character; trademarks may be legally registered by a government, thus obtaining protection for exclusive use in that country. *(p.272)*

11. _____ Packaging that is less harmful to the environment than traditional materials. *(p.277)*

12. _____ The value of a brand to an organization. *(p.273)*

13. _____ A new product sold with the brand name of as a strong existing brand. *(p.273)*

14. _____ Brands that the manufacturer of the product owns. *(p.274)*

15. _____ Agreement in which one firm sells another firm the right to use a brand name for a specific purpose and for a specific period of time. *(p.275)*

MULTIPLE CHOICE

Identify the most correct answer.

1. In some cases, when the existing product line is quite limited, line items are added at both the upper and lower ends, which is a product strategy called a(n): *(p.265)*
   a. downward line stretch.
   b. upward line stretch.
   c. two-way stretch.
   d. filling out strategy.

2. The product mix refers to: *(p.266)*
   a. the set of all products a firm offers for sale.
   b. the number of different versions of each product.
   c. how closely related the items are in terms of technology, end use, channels of distribution, price range, or customer market.
   d. the number of similar products produced by the firm.

3. An individual who is responsible for developing and implementing the marketing plan for all of the brands and products within a product category is a: *(p.278)*
   a. brand manager.
   b. product line manager.
   c. market manager.
   d. product category manager.

4. An individual who is responsible for developing and implementing the marketing plans for products sold to a particular customer group is a: *(p.278)*
    a.   market manager.
    b.   product group manager.
    c.   target manager.
    d.   product line manager.

5. A venture team is: *(p.279)*
    a.   a business formed by two or more companies that agree to pool certain resources for some common purpose.
    b.   groups of people within an organization who work together focusing exclusively on the development of a new product.
    c.   a business formed to introduce products into international markets.
    d.   a business formed by two or more companies for the purpose of developing new products that will benefit both firms.

6. A product line: *(p.264)*
    a.   involves actually designing the product and planning how it will be manufactured.
    b.   means getting individual consumers or organizations that are likely to be future customers to participate in evaluating product benefits during the development stage.
    c.   is a firm's total product offering designed to satisfy a single need or desire of target customers.
    d.   none of the above.

7. In the decline stage of the product life cycle, sales: *(p. 278)*
    a.   decrease.
    b.   increase more slowly than in the past.
    c.   stay the same.
    d.   none of the above.

8. A good brand name fits: *(p.272)*
    a.   the target market.
    b.   the product's benefits and the customer's culture.
    c.   legal requirements.
    d.   all of the above.

9. A new product sold with the same brand name as a strong existing brand is called: *(p.273)*
    a.   inertia.
    b.   brand loyalty.
    c.   brand extension.
    d.   brand equity.

10. A brand that is shared by a group of individual products or individual brands is a(n): *(p.273)*
    a.   extended brand.
    b.   power brand.
    c.   family brand.
    d.   national brand.

11. A family brand: *(p.273)*
    a.   is shared by a group of individual products or individual brands.
    b.   appeals to a narrow segment of the market.
    c.   provides customized benefits that uniquely satisfy consumers.
    d.   all of the above.

12. Brands that are owned by the manufacturer of the product are called: *(p.274)*
    a.   powerful brands.
    b.   segmented brands.
    c.   national or manufacturer brands.
    d.   private brands.

13. Brands that are owned and sold by a specific retailer or distributor are: *(p.274)*
    a.   national brands.
    b.   store or private-label brands.
    c.   manufacturer brands.
    d.   niche or segmented brands.

14. Co-branding: *(p.275)*
    a.   is an agreement between two brands to work together in marketing new or existing products.
    b.   benefits both partners by providing greater recognition power.
    c.   allows for the split of advertising and trade promotion costs.
    d.   all of the above.

15. The covering or container for a product which provides product protection, facilitates product use and storage, and supplies important marketing communication is the: *(p.275)*
    a.   brown wrapper.
    b.   package.
    c.   universal product code.
    d.   product label.

CHAPTER IN REVIEW—WRITING TO LEARN

1.   Explain how product quality is addressed as a product objective.

        _____

        _____

        _____

        _____

2.   Describe how products are managed throughout their life cycle.

        _____

        _____

        _____

3.   Identify the important criteria to be considered in choosing a brand name.

        _____

        _____

        _____

        _____

CASE ANALYSIS

Real People, Real Decisions: Mary Louise Huebner, Canada Cutlery Inc.

Reread the three sections comprising the Canada Cutlery vignette in Chapter 10 and answer the following questions:

1.   What are Canada Cutlery's eight product lines?

2.   What type of agreement did Canada Cutlery have with its European supplier?

3.   Why is branding so important to Canada Cutlery?

4.   What did Canada Cutlery do to protect the new family brand name that it adopted?

SCENARIO

You are a product manager at a Canadian packaged goods company. The Vice President of Marketing has approached you to discuss your next assignment. You are offered the choice of managing four very different products.

Product #1 has just emerged from a successful test market and is ready for broad introduction into the Canadian market. Product #2 was introduced to the market five years ago, and is experiencing a rapid increase in sales. Product #3 has been around for fifteen years. It has a loyal clientele, but sales are beginning to diminish. Product #4 was introduced thirty years ago. Your company is one of only two still manufacturing the product, and a competitor has recently introduced a much improved alternative, which is likely to spell the death knell for your company's offering over the next few years.

1.   If you decide to become Product Manager for Product #1, what will be your main priorities and tasks over the coming year?

2.   If you decide to become Product Manager for Product #2, what will be your main priorities and tasks over the coming year?

3.   If you decide to become Product Manager for Product #3, what will be your main priorities and tasks over the coming year?

4.   If you decide to become Product Manager for Product #4, what will be your main priorities and tasks over the coming year?

ANSWERS

Chapter Outline

I.   CREATING AND NURTURING QUALITY PRODUCTS—Product planning plays a big role in the firm's tactical marketing plans.

II.   USING PRODUCT OBJECTIVES TO DECIDE ON A PRODUCT STRATEGY—Product objectives provide focus and direction.

    A.   Objectives And Strategies For Individual Products—For new products, the objectives relate to successful introduction. For mature products, the objectives may focus on breathing new life into a product.

    B.   Objectives And Strategies For Multiple Products

        1.   Product Line Strategies—A firm's total product offering designed to satisfy a single need or desire of target customers.

            Full-Line Strategy—A large number of variations in a firm's product line.

            Limited-Line Strategy—A firm that markets a smaller number of product variations.

            Stretching The Firm's Product Line—An upward line stretch, a downward line stretch, a two-way stretch, a filling-out strategy, or contracting the product line.

            Cannibalization—The loss of sales of an existing product when a new item in a product line or product family is introduced.

            Product Mix—The total set of all products a firm offers for sale.

    C.   Quality As A Product Objective—Product quality objectives include level and consistency of quality.

III.   MARKETING THROUGHOUT THE PRODUCT LIFE CYCLE—The concept that explains how products go through four distinct stages from birth to death: introduction, growth, maturity, and decline.

    A.   The Introduction Stage—The first stage of the product life cycle, in which slow growth follows the introduction of a new product in the marketplace.

    B.   The Growth Stage—The second stage in the product life cycle, during which the product is accepted and sales rapidly increase.

    C.   The Maturity Stage—The third and longest stage in the product life cycle, in which sales peak and profit margins narrow.

    D.   The Decline Stage—The final stage in the product life cycle, in which sales decrease, as customer needs change.

IV.   CREATING PRODUCT IDENTITY: BRANDING DECISIONS

    A.   What's In a Name (or a Symbol)?

        Brand—A name, a term, a symbol, or any other unique element of a product, which identifies one firm's product(s) and sets them apart from the competition.

        1.   Choosing a Brand Name, Mark, or Character—A good brand is: easy to say, spell, read, and remember. The name should also fit the target market, fit the product's benefits, fit the customer's culture, and fit legal requirements.

        2.   Trademarks—The legal term for a brand name, brand mark, or trade character; trademarks may be legally registered by a government, thus obtaining protection for exclusive use in that country.

    B.   The Importance of Branding

        Brand Equity—The value of a brand to an organization.

        Brand Extension—A new product sold with the same brand name as a strong existing brand.

C. Branding Strategies
1. Individual Brands Versus Family Brands
Individual Brand Strategy—A separate, unique brand for each product item.
Family Brand—Marketing multiple items under the same brand name.
2. National and Store Brands
National or Manufacturer Brands—Brands owned by the manufacturer of the product.
Store or Private Label Brands—Brands owned and sold by a specific retailer or distributor.
3. Licensing—An agreement in which one firm sells another firm the right to use a brand name for a specific purpose and for a specific period of time.
4. Co-Branding—An agreement between two brands to work together in marketing new or existing products.

V. CREATING PRODUCT IDENTITY: PACKAGING AND LABELLING DECISIONS
A. Packaging Functions
Package—The covering or container for a product that provides product protection, facilitates product use and storage, and supplies important marketing communication.
B. Designing Effective Packaging—Packaging material, (Green packaging), Packaging shape, size, etc.
C. Labelling Regulations—The Consumer Packaging and Labelling Act controls package communications and labelling in Canada.

VI. ORGANIZING FOR EFFECTIVE PRODUCT MANAGEMENT
A. Management Of Existing Products—Product management may include brand managers, product category managers, and market managers.
1. Brand Managers—An individual who is responsible for developing and implementing the marketing plan for a single brand.
2. Product Category Manager—An individual who is responsible for developing and implementing the marketing plan for all of the brands and products within a product category.
3. Market Manager—An individual who is responsible for developing and implementing the marketing plans for products sold to a particular customer group.
B. Organizing For New-Product Development—Often individuals who are assigned to manage new-product development are especially creative people with entrepreneurial skills.
Venture Teams—Groups of people within an organization who work together focusing exclusively on the development of a new product.

Key Terms

1. Product line
2. Cannibalization
3. Product mix
4. Brand manager
5. Market manager
6. Venture teams
7. Product life cycle
8. Growth stage
9. Brand
10. Trademark
11. Green packaging
12. Brand equity
13. Brand extensions
14. National or manufacturer brands
15. Licensing

Multiple Choice

1. c
2. a
3. d
4. a
5. b
6. c
7. a
8. d
9. c
10. c
11. a
12. c
13. b
14. d
15. b

Chapter in Review—Writing to Learn

1. Product objectives often address product quality or the ability of the product to satisfy customers. Product quality is tied to customer expectations of product performance. For individual products, quality may mean durability, degree of precision, ease of use and repair, or degree of aesthetic pleasure. Product quality objectives are likely to focus on the level and the consistency of product quality.

2. In the introductory stage, the goal is to get customers to try the product. During growth, firms focus on establishing brand loyalty and may improve the product. In maturity, significant product modification may occur and new users may be attracted with market differentiation strategies. During the decline stage, firms must decide whether to keep the product or to phase it out.

3. Brand names should be easy to say, spell, read and remember and should fit the target market, the product's benefits, the customer's culture, and legal requirements.

Case Analysis

1. Canada Cutlery markets four lines of knives, one line of knife sharpeners, two lines of specialized tools and one line of cutlery carrying cases.

2. The two companies had entered into a co-branding agreement.

3. Branding is particularly important to the company because when chefs start using a specific brand, they generally remain brand-loyal.

4. Canada Cutlery decided to protect its new family brand name by obtaining a trademark for it, in both Canada and the United States.

CHAPTER 11

Broadening the Product Focus: Marketing Intangibles and Services

CHAPTER OVERVIEW

The purpose of this chapter is to describe the characteristics of services and explain marketing of intangibles. Important service characteristics include intangibility (they cannot be seen, touched, or smelled), perishability (they cannot be stored), variability (they are never exactly the same), and inseparability from the product (most services are produced, sold, and consumed at the same time).

The satisfaction of service customers, that is, the perception of service quality, is related to prior expectations and can be measured by gap analysis or critical incident technique. In developing strategies for services, marketers focus on both the core service—the basic benefit received from the service—and on augmented services—innovative features, and unique delivery systems, etc. Sometimes marketing intangibles means packaging, promoting, and selling people such as politicians and celebrities as well as the promotion of causes and ideas, known as cause marketing.

Finally, in marketing intangibles, some important marketing mix elements, such as packaging and labelling, are not relevant. Price is very important in services marketing as an indicator of quality. Promotion, as with the marketing of goods, must focus on different market segments.

CHAPTER OBJECTIVES

1. Explain the marketing of people, places, and ideas.

2. Describe the four characteristics of services, and understand how services differ from goods.

3. Explain how marketers measure service quality.

4. Explain marketing strategies for services and not-for-profit organizations.

CHAPTER OUTLINE

With reference to the textbook, please provide a brief description of each of the main elements listed in the Chapter Outline below. The page numbers will help guide you through the learning process.

I. MARKETING WHAT ISN'T THERE
Intangibles _____ (p.288)
  A. Does Marketing Work For Intangibles? _____ (p.288)
    1. Mission Statement _____ (p.290)
    2. Situation Analysis _____ (p.290)
    3. Product Life Cycle _____ (p.290)
  B. Marketing People, Places, And Ideas
    1. Marketing People
    Pure Selling Approach _____ (p.291)
    Product Improvement Approach _____ (p.291)
    Market Fulfillment Approach _____ (p.291)
    2. Marketing Places _____ (p.291)
    3. Marketing Ideas
    Idea Marketing _____ (p.292)
    Cause Marketing _____ (p.293)

II. WHAT IS A SERVICE?
Services _____ (p.294)
  A. Characteristics of Services
    1. Intangibility _____ (p.295)
    2. Perishability _____ (p.296)
    Capacity Management _____ (p.296)
    3. Variability _____ (p.296)
    4. Inseparability _____ (p.296)
    Service Encounter _____ (p.296)
    Disintermediation _____ (p.296)
  B. The Goods/Services Continuum _____ (p.296)
    1. Good-Dominated Products
    Embodying _____ (p.296)
    2. Equipment- or Facility-Driven Services
    Facility-driven services _____ (p.298)
    Operational Factors _____ (p.298)
    Locational Factors _____ (p.298)
    Environmental Factors _____ (p.298)
    3. People-Based Services _____ (p.299)
  C. Core And Augmented Services
    Core Service _____ (p.299)
    Augmented Services _____ (p.299)

III.   PROVIDING QUALITY SERVICE
    A.   Judging Service Quality_____ *(p.300)*
        1.   Quality is About Exceeding Expectations
           Internal Marketing_____ *(p.301)*
        2.   Evaluative Dimensions Of Service Quality
           Search Qualities _____ *(p.301)*
           Experience Qualities _____ *(p.302)*
           Credence Qualities _____ *(p.302)*
    B.   Measuring Service Quality
        1.   Gap Analysis_____ *(p.303)*
        2.   The Critical Incident Technique _____ *(p.303)*

IV.   STRATEGIES FOR DEVELOPING AND MANAGING SERVICES
    A.   Services As Theatre_____ *(p.304)*
    B.   Targeting And Positioning Strategies For Services
        1.   Targeting: Defining the Service Customer or Audience
           Audience Maintenance _____ *(p.305)*
           Audience Enrichment _____ *(p.305)*
           Audience Expansion _____ *(p.305)*
           Audience Development_____ *(p.305)*
        2.   Positioning: Defining the Service to Customers
           Tangibles_____ *(p.307)*
           Physical Evidence _____ *(p.307)*
           Responsiveness _____ *(p.307)*
           Empathy _____ *(p.307)*
           Assurance _____ *(p.308)*

KEY TERMS

Select the correct term for each definition and write it in the space provided.

Augmented services	Gap analysis
Core service	Service encounter
Empathy	Capacity management
Embodying	Idea marketing
Services	Disintermediation
Physical evidence	Critical incident technique
Assurance	Cause marketing
Internal marketing	

1. _____ Intangible products that are exchanged directly from producer to customer. *(p.295)*

2. _____ The actual interaction between the customer and the service provider. *(p.296)*

3. _____ Marketing activities aimed at employees in an effort to inform them about the firm's offerings and their high quality. *(p.301)*

4. _____ A marketing research methodology that measures the difference between a customer's expectation of service quality and what actually occurred. *(p.303)*

5. _____ A method of measuring service quality in which customer complaints are used to identify critical incidents, specific face-to-face contacts between consumers and service providers that cause problems and lead to dissatisfaction. *(p.303)*

6. _____ The basic benefit that is obtained as a result of having a service performed. *(p.299)*

7. _____ The core service plus additional services provided to enhance value. *(p.299)*

8. _____ The process of eliminating interaction between customers and salespeople. *(p.294)*

9. _____ An organization that emphasizes the knowledge or competence of its employees. *(p.308)*

10. _____ The inclusion of a service with a purchase of a physical good. *(p.297)*

11. _____ Marketing activities that seek to gain market share for a concept, philosophy, belief, or issue. *(p.292)*

12. _____ A visible signal that communicates not only a product's quality but also the product's desired market position to the consumer. *(p.307)*

13. _____ The process by which organizations adjust their offerings in an attempt to match demand. *(p.296)*

14. _____ An organization that says it understands its customers' needs and genuinely cares about their welfare expresses: *(p.307)*

15. _____ Commercial marketing efforts that are linked to a charitable cause. *(p.293)*

MULTIPLE CHOICE

Identify the most correct answer.

1. All services share the following characteristics that make them distinct from physical products: *(p.295)*
   a. Intangibility, perishability, inseparability, and variability.
   b. Tangibility, inseparability, variability, and durability.
   c. Tangibility, perishability, durability, and variability.
   d. Intangibility, perishability, inseparability, and durability.

2. Service intangibility means that: *(p.295)*
   a. services can't be stored.
   b. the same service activities are performed in different ways from one day to the next.
   c. customers can't see, touch, or smell good service.
   d. both the customer and the service provider must be present at the same time for the service to be delivered.

3. The strategy of including a service with the sale of a physical good is termed: *(p.297)*
   a. service continuum.
   b. embodying.
   c. variability.
   d. resourcing.

4. Facility-driven services, such as automatic car washes, amusement parks, museums, movie theaters, health clubs, tanning salons, and zoos, must be concerned with the following important factors: *(p.298)*
    a. Operational factors.
    b. Locational factors.
    c. Environmental factors.
    d. All of the above.

5. Search qualities that a customer can use to choose among products refer to: *(p.302)*
    a. product characteristics that can only be determined during or after consumption.
    b. attributes that are difficult to evaluate even after we've experienced them.
    c. attributes that the consumer can examine prior to purchase.
    d. techniques that can be used to provide insights on service satisfaction.

6. Some major gaps identified during gap analysis include: *(p.303)*
    a. Management understands what the customer's expectations are.
    b. Management fails to establish a quality control program.
    c. Employees deliver the service at the level specified by the company.
    d. All of the above.

7. Specific face-to-face contacts between consumers and service providers that cause problems and lead to dissatisfaction are called: *(p.303)*
    a. critical incidents.
    b. unreasonable demands.
    c. unrealistic expectations.
    d. cause marketing.

8. An example of augmented services that an airline may offer is: *(p.299)*
    a. safe transportation from point A to point B.
    b. frequent flyer miles.
    c. arriving intact at your destination.
    d. none the above.

9. Experience-based products that cannot be touched are called: *(p.288)*
    a. standardized services.
    b. tangibles.
    c. intangibles.
    d. tangible services.

10. Many companies feel that the best way to bring about social change is through: *(p.293)*
    a. idea marketing.
    b. theory marketing.
    c. influence marketing.
    d. cause marketing.

11. An example from the back stage region of a service performance for a fancy restaurant is: *(p.304)*
    a. appropriate music playing softly in the background.
    b. the kitchen where the food is prepared.
    c. tables that are clean and elegantly set.
    d. flaming delicacies brought to the table.

12. Idea marketing seeks to gain market share for a: *(p.292)*
    a. concept, philosophy, belief, or issue.
    b. theory, belief, view, or opinion.
    c. philosophy, theory, opinion, or belief.
    d. issue, opinion, theory, or belief.

13. The electric company, knowing that demand for its service will rise systematically as the temperature goes up, undertakes: *(p.296)*
    a. demand management.
    b. standardized service.
    c. capacity management.
    d. cause marketing.

14. Organizations that try to attract visitors (and their dollars) to a site, whether a resort, theme park, or city, are engaging in: *(p.292)*
    a. tourism marketing.
    b. organization marketing.
    c. target marketing.
    d. brand marketing.

15. Like other products, celebrities even rename themselves to craft a: *(p.291)*
    a. market target.
    b. brand target.
    c. brand market.
    d. brand identity.

CHAPTER IN REVIEW—WRITING TO LEARN

1. Describe the characteristics of services.

    _____

    _____

    _____

    _____

2.   Explain how marketers evaluate service quality.

_____

_____

_____

_____

3.   Explain the marketing of not-for-profit organizations.

_____

_____

_____

_____

CASE ANALYSIS

Real People, Real Decisions: Vaughn McIntyre and Susan Brekelmans, Charity.ca

Reread the three sections comprising the Charity.ca vignette in Chapter 11 and answer the following questions:

1.   What is Charity.ca's core service? What is its augmented service?

2.   Which target markets did the company initially consider targeting?

3.   What type of marketing is Charity.ca engaged in?

4.   Where does Charity.ca fall on the goods-services continuum?

SCENARIO

You've just graduated with a business degree and have decided to open an eat-in restaurant specializing in pizza. You also plan to offer takeout service, as there is a significant student population nearby. You've leased a 2000 square foot ground floor space, and have hired a well-known chef who specializes in the creation of gourmet pizzas.

You recall from your marketing course that the marketing of services can be challenging—and already, you find yourself faced with a million decisions. You decide to call your marketing teacher, and ask her if she has any advice. She suggests you reread Chapter 11 of your marketing text, and do the following:

1. Draw a figure showing your core and augmented services, using Figure 11.2 on page 299 as your guide. This will help you determine the scope of your offering, and guide you with respect to where should put your efforts and resources.
2. Develop an *internal marketing* strategy, as described on page 301.
3. Decide how you will measure service quality—take a look at the gap analysis and critical incident techniques discussed in your text.
4. How will you target and position your restaurant?

ANSWERS

Chapter Outline

I.   MARKETING WHAT ISN'T THERE
      Intangibles—Experience-based products that cannot be touched.
      A.   Does Marketing Work for Intangibles?—Yes, if the basics of developing a strategic plan are applied.
            1.   Mission Statement—Should include concrete goals.
            2.   Situation Analysis—An assessment of environmental threats and opportunities.
            3.   Product Life Cycle—The organization's goals must consider which part of the product life cycle it is in.
      B.   Marketing People, Places, and Ideas
            1.   Marketing People
                  Pure Selling Approach—The agent presents a client's qualifications to potential "buyers" until he or she finds one who is willing to act as an intermediary.
                  Product Improvement Approach—The agent works with the client to modify certain characteristics that will increase market value.
                  Market Fulfillment Approach—The agent scans the market to identify unmet needs.
            2.   Marketing Places—In tourism marketing, organizations try to attract visitors (and their dollars) to a site, resort, theme park, or city.
            3.   Marketing Ideas
                  Idea Marketing—Marketing activities that seek to gain market share for a concept, philosophy, belief, or issue by using elements of the marketing mix to create or change a target market's attitude or behaviour.
                  Cause Marketing—Commercial marketing efforts that are linked to a charitable cause.

II.   WHAT IS A SERVICE?
      Services—Intangible products that are exchanged directly from producer to the customer.
      A.   Characteristics of Services
            1.   Intangibility—Customers can't see, touch, or smell good service.
            2.   Perishability—Firms can't store its services; they must "use it or lose it".
                  Capacity Management—The process by which the offering is adjusted in an attempt to match demand.
            3.   Variability—The inevitable differences in a service provider's performance from one day to the next.
            4.   Inseparability—A service can only take place at the time the service provider performs an act on either the customer or the customer's possession.
                  Service Encounter—The actual interaction between the customer and the service provider.
                  Disintermediation—The process of eliminating interaction between customers and salespeople.
      B.   The Goods/Services Continuum—Most products are a combination of goods and services.
            1.   Good-Dominated Products
                  Embodying—The inclusion of a service with a purchase of a physical good.
            2.   Equipment- Or Facility-Based Services
                  Facility-driven services—Include three important factors that must be considered.
                  Operational Factors—Technologies that show customers how to use a service, as well as move them smoothly through it.
                  Locational Factors—How far the service is from purchasers.
                  Environmental Factors—Creation of an attractive environment to lure customers into the location.
            3.   People-Based Services—Because people have less and less time to perform various tasks.

C.   Core And Augmented Services

          Core Service—The basic benefit that is obtained as a result of having a service performed.

          Augmented Services—The core service plus additional services provided to enhance value.

III.   PROVIDING QUALITY SERVICE

      A.   Judging Service Quality—Satisfaction or dissatisfaction is more than a reaction to the actual performance quality.

          1.   Quality is About Exceeding Expectations

                Internal Marketing—Marketing activities aimed at employees, to sell them on the idea that they work for a superior company of which they can be proud.

          2.   Evaluative Dimensions Of Service Quality

                Search Qualities—The attributes that the consumer can examine prior to purchase

                Experience Qualities—Product characteristics that customers can determine during or after consumption.

                Credence Qualities—Attributes we find difficult to evaluate even after we've experienced them.

      B.   Measuring Service Quality

          1.   Gap Analysis—A marketing research methodology that measures the difference between a customer's expectation of service quality and what actually occurred.

          2.   The Critical Incident Technique—A method for measuring service quality in which customer complaints are used to identify critical incidents, specific face-to-face contacts between consumers and service providers that cause problems and lead to dissatisfaction.

IV.   STRATEGIES FOR DEVELOPING AND MANAGING SERVICES

      A.   Services As Theatre—A service performance often takes place in two areas, the back stage and the front stage.

      B.   Targeting And Positioning Strategies For Services

          1.   Targeting: Defining The Service Customer Or Audience.

                Audience Maintenance—Goal is to deepen their commitment to the organization.

                Audience Enrichment—Goal is to enhance the experience of attendees to ensure their ongoing loyalty to the organization.

                Audience Expansion—Goal is to increase the number of people who attend.

                Audience Development—Goal is to convince non-attendees that they would enjoy the event.

          2.   Positioning: Defining The Service To Customers

                Tangibles—Services often rely heavily on physical evidence.

                Physical Evidence—A visible signal that communicates not only a product's quality, but also the product's desired market position to the consumer.

                Responsiveness—Speed and care with which firms respond to customers' requests.

                Empathy—Organization understands a customer's needs and genuinely cares about their welfare.

                Assurance—Knowledge or competence of its employees.

Key Terms

1. Services
2. Service encounter
3. Internal marketing
4. Gap analysis
5. Critical incident technique
6. Core service
7. Augmented services
8. Disintermediation
9. Assurance
10. Embodying
11. Idea marketing
12. Physical evidence
13. Capacity management
14. Empathy
15. Cause marketing

Multiple Choice

1.	a
2.	c
3.	b
4.	d
5.	c
6.	b
7.	a
8.	b
9.	c
10.	d
11.	b
12.	a
13.	c
14.	a
15.	d

Chapter in Review—Writing To Learn

1. Important service characteristics include 1) intangibility (they cannot be seen, or touched, or smelled), 2) perishability (they cannot be stored), 3) variability (they are never exactly the same) and 4) inseparability from the producer (most services are produced, sold, and consumed at the same time).

2. Both qualitative and quantitative research methods may be used to measure customer satisfaction. Gap analysis measures the difference between customer expectations of service quality and what actually occurred. Using a critical incident technique, service firms can identify the specific contacts between customers and service providers that create dissatisfaction.

3. Not-for-profit organizations also develop marketing strategies to "sell" social services, cultural experiences, ideas such as environmental protection, or a political or religious philosophy.

Case Analysis

1. Charity.ca's core service is the ability to facilitate online donations to charities. Its augmented services include information on charitable giving and links to charities.

2. The three target markets were: 20-30 year olds, 30-54 year olds with higher incomes, and seniors.

3. Charity.ca is engaged in idea marketing.

4. Charity.ca is a pure service provider.

CHAPTER 12

Pricing the Product

CHAPTER OVERVIEW

In this chapter, we learned the importance of pricing. Price, the amount of outlay of money, goods, services or deeds given in exchange for a product, may be monetary, such as dues and rent, or nonmonetary, such as a vote for a candidate and contribution for time.

Demand is the amount of a product customers are willing to buy at different prices. Price elasticity of demand is the sensitivity of customers to changing prices. With elastic demand, changes in price create large changes in demand. When demand is inelastic, increases in price have little effect on demand, so that total revenue increases.

Break-even analysis uses fixed and variable costs to identify how many units will have to be sold at a certain price in order to begin making a profit. Marginal analysis uses both costs and estimates of product demand to identify the price that will maximize profits.

Finally, like other elements of the marketing mix, pricing is influenced by a variety of external environmental factors. This includes economic trends such as inflation and recession, and the firm's competitive environment, that is, whether the firm does business in an oligopoly, monopoly, or a more competitive environment.

CHAPTER OBJECTIVES

1. Explain the importance of pricing and how prices can take both monetary and nonmonetary forms.

2. Understand the pricing objectives that marketers typically have in planning pricing strategies.

3. Explain how customer demand influences pricing decisions.

4. Describe how marketers use costs, demands, and revenue to make pricing decisions.

5. Understand some of the environmental factors that affect pricing strategies.

CHAPTER OUTLINE

With reference to the textbook, please provide a brief description of each of the main elements listed in the Chapter Outline below. The page numbers will help guide you through the learning process.

I.   "YES, BUT WHAT DOES IT COST?"
      A.   Monetary and Nonmonetary Prices
            Price _____ *(p.320)*
            Bartering _____ *(p.321)*
            Operating Costs _____ *(p.321)*
            Switching Costs _____ *(p.321)*
            Opportunity Cost _____ *(p.321)*
      B.   The Importance of Pricing Decisions _____ *(p.322)*
      C.   Pricing and the Marketing Mix
            1.   Price and Distribution _____ *(p.322)*
            2.   Price and Product _____ *(p.323)*
            3.   Price and Communications _____ *(p.323)*

II.   DEVELOPING PRICING OBJECTIVES _____ *(p.324)*
      A.   Sales or Market Share Objectives _____ *(p.325)*
      B.   Profit Objectives _____ *(p.325)*
      C.   Competitive Effect Objectives _____ *(p.326)*
      D.   Customer Satisfaction Objectives _____ *(p.326)*
      E.   Image Enhancement Objectives _____ *(p.326)*
      F.   Flexibility of Price Objectives _____ *(p.327)*

III.   ESTIMATING DEMAND: HOW DEMAND
      INFLUENCES PRICING _____ *(p.327)*
      A.   Demand Curves _____ *(p.327)*
            Law of Demand _____ *(p.327)*
            1.   Shifts in Demand _____ *(p.327)*
            2.   Estimating Demand_____ *(p.328)*
      B.   The Price Elasticity of Demand_____ *(p.329)*
            1.   Elastic and Inelastic Demand
                  Elastic Demand _____ *(p.330)*
                  Inelastic Demand_____ *(p.330)*
            2.   Influences on Demand Elasticity_____ *(p.332)*
                  Income Effect _____ *(p.332)*

IV.   DETERMINING COST
    A.   Types of Costs _____ *(p.334)*
        1.   Variable Costs _____ *(p.334)*
        2.   Fixed Costs _____ *(p.334)*
        3.   Total Costs _____ *(p.335)*
    B.   Break-Even Analysis _____ *(p.335)*
    C.   Marginal Analysis _____ *(p.337)*
        Marginal Cost _____ *(p.337)*
        Marginal Revenue _____ *(p.337)*

V.   EVALUATING THE PRICING ENVIRONMENT _____ *(p.339)*
    A.   The Economy _____ *(p.339)*
        1.   Trimming the Fat: Pricing in a Recession _____ *(p.339)*
        2.   Increasing Prices: Responding to Inflation _____ *(p.340)*
    B.   The Competition _____ *(p.340)*
    C.   Consumer Trends_____ *(p.341)*
    D.   International Environmental Influences _____ *(p.341)*
        Price Subsidies_____ *(p.342)*

KEY TERMS

Select the correct term for each definition and write it in the space provided.

Marginal analysis	Price elasticity of demand
Bartering	Inferior goods
Price subsidies	Marginal revenue
Fixed costs	Marginal cost
Price	Total costs
Cross-elasticity of demand	Operating costs
Substitute	Break-Even Analysis
Variable costs	

1.   _____   The value that customers give up, or exchange, to obtain a desired product. *(p.320)*

2.   _____   The practice of exchanging a good or service for another good or service of like value. *(p.321)*

3.   _____   Costs involved in using a product. *(p.321)*

4. _____ A measure of the sensitivity of customers to changes in price; the percentage change in unit sales that result from a percentage change in price. *(p.330)*

5. _____ The costs of production that are tied to and vary depending on the number of units produced; variable costs typically include raw materials, processed materials, component parts and labour. *(p.334)*

6. _____ Costs of production that do not change with the number of units produced. *(p.334)*

7. _____ The total of the fixed costs and the variable costs for a set number of units produced. *(p.335)*

8. _____ A method for determining the number of units which will have to be produced and sold at a given price to break even, i.e., to neither make a profit nor suffer a loss. *(p.335)*

9. _____ A method of analysis that uses cost and demand to identify the price that will maximize profits. *(p.337)*

10. _____ The increase in total cost that results from producing one additional unit of a product. *(p.337)*

11. _____ When changes in the prices of other products affect the demand for a given item. *(p.332)*

12. _____ For some goods, as your income increases, your demand decreases. *(p.332)*

13. _____ A product that can satisfy the demand of another product. *(p.332)*

14. _____ Government payments made to protect domestic businesses or to reimburse them when they must price at or below cost to make a sale. *(p.342)*

15. _____ The increase in total revenue (income) that results from producing and selling one additional unit of a product. *(p.337)*

MULTIPLE CHOICE

Identify the most correct answer.

1. The value of something that is given up to obtain something else is called: *(p.320)*
   a. bartering.
   b. a cost-value relationship.
   c. a professional fee.
   d. opportunity cost.

2. Costs involved in moving from one brand to another are called: *(p.321)*
   a. opportunity costs.
   b. switching costs.
   c. operating costs.
   d. fixed costs.

3. What classification of pricing objectives (and strategies) is tailored to different geographic areas and time periods? *(p. 327)*
   a. flexibility of price objectives.
   b. image enhancement objectives.
   c. profit objectives.
   d. sales or market share objectives.

4. If prices decrease, customers will buy more. This is known as the: *(p.327)*
   a. income effect on demand.
   b. backward-bending demand.
   c. law of demand.
   d. consumer pricing sensitivity.

5. In the simplest terms, price elasticity of demand is calculated as follows: *(p.330)*
   a. Percentage change in price divided by percentage change in quantity.
   b. Percentage change in quantity divided by percentage change in price.
   c. Percentage change in quantity multiplied by percentage change in price.
   d. Percentage change in price subtracted from percentage change in quantity.

6.   When a percentage change in price results in a large percentage change in quantity demanded, demand is said to be: *(p.330)*
   a.   price elastic.
   b.   cross-elastic.
   c.   price inelastic.
   d.   fixed.

7.   Fixed costs include: *(p.334)*
   a.   raw materials.
   b.   labour.
   c.   rent or the cost of owning and maintaining the factory.
   d.   all of the above.

8.   At the break-even point: *(p.335)*
   a.   marketers can identify how many units of a product have to be sold to make money.
   b.   revenue or income from sales are just equal to costs.
   c.   variable costs equal fixed costs.
   d.   none the above.

9.   The contribution per unit is calculated as: *(p.336)*
   a.   total fixed costs divided by variable costs.
   b.   the difference between the total fixed costs and the variable costs.
   c.   the sum of the total fixed cost and the target profit per unit.
   d.   the difference between what a firm sells a product for (the revenue per unit) and the variable costs.

10.   The increase in total revenue (income) that results from producing and selling one additional unit of a product is called: *(p.337)*
   a.   marginal revenue.
   b.   revenue goal.
   c.   marginal cost.
   d.   per-unit profit.

11.   When customers are very sensitive to changes in prices, and a change in price results in a substantial change in the quantity demanded, this is called: *(p.330)*
   a.   inelastic demand.
   b.   sensitivity demand.
   c.   quality demand.
   d.   elastic demand.

12.   The _____ effect on demand means that changes in your earnings affect demand for a product, even if its price remains the same. *(p.332)*
   a.   substitution.
   b.   price.
   c.   income.
   d.   earnings.

13. Products such as clothing and housing are examples of: *(p.332)*
    a. normal goods.
    b. inferior goods.
    c. superior goods.
    d. staple goods.

14. The increase in total cost that results from producing one additional unit of a product is: *(p.337)*
    a. marginal analysis.
    b. marginal revenue.
    c. marginal income.
    d. marginal cost.

15. In addition to demand and costs, factors in the firm's _____ environment are important to making successful pricing decisions: *(p.338)*
    a. demand.
    b. international.
    c. internal.
    d. external.

CHAPTER IN REVIEW—WRITING TO LEARN

1. Explain how price can take both monetary and nonmonetary forms.

    _____

    _____

    _____

2. Describe the concept of price elasticity of demand.

    _____

    _____

    _____

3.   Describe the pricing objectives that marketers typically have in planning pricing strategies.

_____

_____

_____

_____

CASE ANALYSIS

Real People, Real Decisions: Meet Astrid de Bruyn, Palliser Furniture Ltd.

Reread the three sections comprising the Palliser Furniture vignette in Chapter 12 and answer the following questions:

1.   Which reasons did retailers and Palliser sales representatives proffer for the poor sales of Palliser's new "membrane press" product line?

2.   Which pricing options did Astrid de Bruyn consider?

3.   What impact might lowering the price have on retailers that had already purchased the product at the higher price level?

4.   What impact would leaving the price "as is" have on de Bruyn's marketing strategy?

SCENARIO

Your marketing teacher recently told you about a new invention—a pop dispensing machine which, when placed outdoors, can actually sense the temperature of the outside air and change the price of the pop automatically. When the outside temperature is high, the price of pop goes up. When the outside temperature is low, the price of pop goes down. Your first reaction is amazement, but then, your marketing teacher starts to give you all kinds of examples of situations much like this one: restaurant meals costing less at lunch than in the evening, movies costing less on Tuesdays, and so forth. He asks you the following:

1.   In what way does this new invention capitalize on the demand curve?
2.   What role does price elasticity play in the probable success of the dispensing machine?
3.   Which pricing objectives—sales, market share, profit, competitive, customer satisfaction or image enhancement—does this invention support?
4.   How does this invention accommodate shifts in demand?

ANSWERS

Chapter Outline

I. "YES, BUT WHAT DOES IT COST?"
    A. Monetary and Nonmonetary Prices
        Price—The value that customers give up or exchange to obtain a desired product.
        Bartering—The practice of exchanging a good or service for another good or service of like value.
        Operating Costs—Costs involved in using a product.
        Switching Costs—Costs involved in moving from one brand to another.
        Opportunity Cost—The value of something that is given up to obtain something else.
    B. The Importance of Pricing Decisions—Pricing is probably the least understood and least appreciated element of the marketing mix.
    C. Pricing and the Marketing Mix
        1. Price and Distribution—Pricing decisions must be considered from the viewpoint of each member of the channel of distribution—the manufacturers, wholesalers, and retailers—that help get the product to consumers.
        2. Price and Product—The price of the product must cover the costs of doing business, but price also sends a signal about product quality. The stage of the product's life cycle also affects pricing.
        3. Price and Communication—It is important that the advertising strategies justify the cost of the product.
        4. Price and Relationship Management—High-priced products often have sufficient margins to support a closer and more responsive relationship with customers.

II. DEVELOPING PRICING OBJECTIVES—Pricing objectives must support the broader objectives of the firm (such as maximizing shareholder value) as well as its overall marketing objectives (such as increasing market share).
    A. Sales or Market Share Objectives—Often the objective of pricing strategy is to maximize sales (in dollars or in units) or to increase market share.
    B. Profit Objectives—A profit objective focuses on a target level of profit growth or a desired net profit margin.
    C. Competitive Effect Objectives—The pricing plan is intended to have a certain effect on the marketing efforts of the competition.
    D. Customer Satisfaction Objectives—Many quality-focused firms believe that profits result from making customer satisfaction the primary objective, and set price to offer maximum value to the customer.
    E. Image Enhancement Objectives—Price is often an important means of communicating not only quality, but also image to prospective customers.
    F. Flexibility of Price Objectives—Often it is necessary to develop pricing objectives (and strategies) tailored to different geographic areas and time periods.

III. ESTIMATING DEMAND: HOW DEMAND INFLUENCES PRICING—Demand is customers' desire for products.
    A. Demand Curves—Show the quality of a product that customers will buy in a market during a period of time at various prices if all other factors remain the same.
        The Law of Demand—As the price of the product goes up, the number of units that customers are willing to buy goes down. If price decreases, customers will buy more.
        1. Shifts in Demand—An upward shift in the demand curve means that, at any given price, demand is greater than before the shift occurs.
        2. Estimating Demand—All marketing planning and budgeting must be based on reasonably accurate estimates of potential sales.

B.   The Price Elasticity of Demand—The percentage change in unit sales that results from a percentage change in price.

1.   Elastic and Inelastic Demand

Elastic Demand—Customers who are very sensitive to changes in prices, and a change in price results in a substantial change in the quantity demanded.

Inelastic Demand—A change in price has little or no effect on the quantity that consumers are willing to buy and demand.

2.   Influences on Demand Elasticity—If a product has a close substitute, its demand will be elastic; that is, a change in price will result in a change in demand, as consumers move to buy the substitute product.

Income Effect—Changes in income affect demand for a product, even if its price remains the same.

III.   DETERMINING COST

A.   Types of Costs—How much the price exceeds the cost determines the amount of profit the firm may earn, everything else being equal.

1.   Variable Costs—The costs of production (raw and processed materials, parts, and labour) that are tied to, and vary depending on, the number of units produced.

2.   Fixed Costs—Costs of production that do not change with the number of units produced.

3.   Total Costs—The total of the fixed costs and the variable costs for a set number of units produced.

B.   Break-Even Analysis—A method for determining the number of units that a firm must produce and sell at a given price to cover all its costs.

C.   Marginal Analysis—A method that uses cost and demand to identify the price that will maximize profits.

Marginal Cost—The increase in total cost that results from producing one additional unit of a product.

Marginal Revenue—The increase in total revenue (income) that results from producing and selling one additional unit of a product.

IV.   EVALUATING THE PRICING ENVIRONMENT—An understanding of the factors in the firm's external environment are important to make successful pricing decisions.

A.   The Economy—The business cycle, inflation, economic growth, and consumer confidence all help to determine whether one pricing strategy or another will succeed.

1.   Trimming the Fat: Pricing in a Recession—During recessions, consumers grow more price sensitive.

2.   Increasing Prices: Responding to Inflation—Economic trends also influence a firm's ability to increase prices because they affect what consumers see as an acceptable or unacceptable price range for a product.

B.   The Competition—Decision makers must worry constantly about how the competition will respond to their pricing actions.

C.   Consumer Trends—Culture and demographics determine how consumers think and behave and so have a large impact on all marketing decisions.

D.   International Environmental Influences—The currency exchange rate influences pricing decisions by firms.

Price Subsidies—Government payments made to protect domestic businesses or to reimburse them when they must price at or below cost to make a sale. The subsidy can be a cash payment or tax relief.

Key Terms

1. Price
2. Bartering
3. Operation costs
4. Price elasticity of demand
5. Variable costs
6. Fixed costs
7. Total costs
8. Break-even analysis
9. Marginal analysis
10. Marginal cost
11. Cross-elasticity of demand
12. Inferior goods
13. Substitute
14. Price subsidies
15. Marginal revenue

Multiple Choice

1. d
2. b
3. a
4. c
5. b
6. a
7. c
8. b
9. d
10. a
11. d
12. c
13. a
14. d
15. d

Chapter in Review—Writing To Learn

1. Price, the amount of outlay of money, goods, services or deeds given in exchange for a product may be monetary (e.g., dues, tuition, professional fee, rent, donations, etc.) or nonmonetary (e.g., a vote for a candidate, contribution of time or effort).

2. Price elasticity of demand is the sensitivity of customers to changing prices. With elastic demand, changes in price create large changes in demand while when demand is inelastic, increases in price have little effect on demand so that total revenue increases.

3. Effective pricing objectives are designed to support corporate and marketing objectives and are flexible. Pricing objectives often focus on sales (to maximize sales or to increase market share), or they may specify a desired level of profit growth or profit margin. At other times, firms may develop pricing objectives for competitive effect, to increase customer satisfaction, or to communicate a certain image to prospective customers. Pricing objectives need to be flexible to adapt to different geographic areas and time periods.

Case Analysis

1. Reasons given for the poor sales included: the series was too contemporary, the product required some limited assembly, and the price points were higher.

2. Ms de Bruyn considered either leaving the pricing "as is" or raising the price.

3. Retailers who had previously purchased the product at the higher price would expect discounts on the inventory they already held, and may feel they had been overcharged previously, causing them to question Palliser's overall approach to pricing.

4. The marketing strategy would require refocusing to support the enhanced value positioning.

CHAPTER 13

Pricing Methods

CHAPTER OVERVIEW

Effective pricing objectives are designed to support corporate and marketing objectives and are flexible. Like other elements in the marketing mix, pricing is influenced by a variety of external environmental factors including economic trends, the firm's competitive environment, changing cultural and demographic consumer trends, and the differences in the costs faced in different markets.

The most common types of pricing strategies are based on cost. Cost-based strategies include cost-plus pricing and price floor pricing. Pricing strategies that are based on demand require that marketers estimate the elasticity of demand in order to be assured they can sell what they produce. Specific strategies include demand backward pricing and chain-markup pricing. Strategies based on the competition may represent industry wisdom but can be tricky due to the responses of competitive firms. Examples of competition-based strategies include price leader strategy, parity pricing strategy, and limit pricing. Firms that focus on customer needs in developing pricing strategies may consider every-day-low-price or value pricing strategies, negotiated pricing policies, two-part pricing, or payment pricing. For multiple products, marketers may use price bundling or captive product pricing.

Pricing for members of the channel may include quantity discounts to encourage larger purchases, cash discounts to encourage fast payment, and seasonal discounts to spread purchases throughout the year or to increase in-season sales. Finally, geographic pricing tactics address differences in how far products must be shipped.

CHAPTER OBJECTIVES

1. Understand key pricing strategies.

2. Explain pricing tactics for individual and multiple products.

3. Describe the psychological aspects of pricing.

4. Understand some of the legal and ethical considerations in pricing.

CHAPTER OUTLINE

With reference to the textbook, please provide a brief description of each of the main elements listed in the Chapter Outline below. The page numbers will help guide you through the learning process.

I.   PRICE PLANNING: MOVE AND COUNTERMOVE _____ *(p.350)*

II.   PRICING STRATEGIES _____ *(p.350)*
      A.   Pricing Strategies Based on Cost_____ *(p.351)*
            1.   Cost-Plus Pricing_____ *(p.351)*
            2.   Price-Floor Pricing _____ *(p.352)*
      B.   Pricing Strategies Based on Demand _____ *(p.353)*
            1.   Demand-Backward Pricing_____ *(p.353)*
            2.   Chain-Markup Pricing_____ *(p.354)*
      C.   Pricing Strategies Based on the Competition
            Price Leader_____ *(p.354)*
      D.   Pricing Strategies Based on Customers' Needs
            Value Pricing, or Everyday Low Pricing (EDLP) _____ *(p.355)*
      E.   New-Product Pricing
            1.   Skimming Price_____ *(p.356)*
            2.   Penetration Pricing _____ *(p.357)*
            3.   Trial Pricing _____ *(p.357)*

III.   DEVELOPING PRICING TACTICS
      A.   Pricing For Individual Products
            1.   Two-Part Pricing_____ *(p.359)*
            2.   Payment Pricing _____ *(p.359)*
      B.   Pricing For Multiple Products
            1.   Price Bundling_____ *(p.359)*
            2.   Captive Pricing _____ *(p.359)*
      C.   Geographic Pricing
            1.   F.O.B. Pricing
                F.O.B. Origin Pricing _____ *(p.359)*
                F.O.B. Delivered Pricing_____ *(p.359)*
            2.   Zone Pricing _____ *(p.360)*
            3.   Uniform Delivered Pricing _____ *(p.360)*
            4.   Freight Absorption Pricing _____ *(p.360)*
      D.   Discounting For Members of The Channel
            1.   Trade or Functional Discounts
                List Price _____ *(p.361)*
                Trade or Functional Discounts _____ *(p.361)*

2.   Quantity Discounts _____ *(p.361)*
           Cumulative Quantity Discounts _____ *(p.361)*
           Noncumulative Quantity Discounts _____ *(p.361)*
3.   Cash Discounts _____ *(p.362)*
4.   Seasonal Discounts _____ *(p.362)*
E.   Pricing With Electronic Commerce_____ *(p.362)*

IV.   PSYCHOLOGICAL ISSUES IN PRICING
    A.   Buyers' Pricing Expectations
         1.   Internal Reference Prices _____ *(p.363)*
         2.   Price-Quality Inferences _____ *(p.363)*
    B.   Psychological Pricing Strategies
         1.   Odd-Even Pricing _____ *(p.364)*
         2.   Price Lining_____ *(p.364)*

V.   LEGAL AND ETHICAL CONSIDERATIONS IN PRICING
    A.   Deceptive Pricing Practices
         Bait-and-Switch_____ *(p.366)*
    B.   Competition Act
         Predatory Pricing_____ *p. 366)*
         Loss Leader Pricing_____ *(p.367)*
    C.   Price Discrimination _____ *(p.367)*
    D.   Price Maintenance or Fixing _____ *(p.367)*
         Horizontal Price Fixing _____ *(p.367)*
         Vertical Price Fixing _____ *(p.367)*

KEY TERMS

Select the correct term for each definition and write it in the space provided.

Price bundling
Chain-markup pricing
Price-floor pricing
Cumulative quantity discounts
Quantity discounts
Skimming price
Captive pricing
Zone pricing

Parity pricing
Trial pricing
Price leader
List price
Demand-based pricing
Penetration pricing
Cost-plus pricing

1. _____ A very high, premium price that a firm charges for its new, highly desirable product. *(p.356)*

2. _____ Pricing a new product low for a limited period of time in order to lower the risk for a customer. *(p.357)*

3. _____ A method of setting prices in which the seller adds up all the costs for the product and then adds the desired profit per unit. *(p.351)*

4. _____ A method for calculating price in which a portion of a firm's output may be sold at a price which only covers marginal costs of production in order to maintain full plant operating capacity. *(p.352)*

5. _____ A method of setting prices which is based on estimates of demand at different prices. *(p.353)*

6. _____ A pricing strategy that extends demand-backward pricing from the ultimate consumer all the way back through channel of distribution to the manufacturer. *(p.354)*

7. _____ The firm that sets price first in an industry; other major firms in the industry follow the leader by staying in line. *(p.354)*

8. _____ A pricing tactic in which customers in different geographic zones pay different transportation rates. *(p.361)*

9. _____ A pricing strategy in which a firm tries to keep its price about equal to its competitors' prices. *(p.354)*

10. _____ Discounts based on the total quantity bought within a specified time period. *(p.361)*

11. _____ A pricing strategy in which a new product is introduced at a very low price in order to encourage more customers to purchase the new product. *(p.357)*

12. _____ Selling two or more goods or services as a single package for one price. *(p.359)*

13. _____ A pricing tactic for two items that must be used together; one item is priced very low and the firm makes its profit on another high-margin item essential to the operation of the first item. *(p.359)*

14. _____ The price the end-customer is expected to pay as determined by the manufacturer. *(p.361)*

15. _____ A pricing strategy of charging reduced prices for purchases of larger quantities of a product. *(p.363)*

MULTIPLE CHOICE

Identify the most correct answer.

1. A price leadership strategy is usually found in a(n): *(p.354)*
   a. monopoly.
   b. oligopoly.
   c. democracy.
   d. dictatorship.

2. Generally, firms that do business in an oligopoly are likely to: *(p.354)*
   a. adopt status quo pricing objectives in which pricing is linked to the competition.
   b. focus on nonprice competition.
   c. price each product based on its cost without much concern for matching the exact price of the competitors' products.
   d. focus on more value for the same price as the competition.

3. If the prices (and other characteristics) of two products are fairly close, it is likely that the consumer will feel the product quality is similar. This is called: *(p.363)*
   a. a price/quality relationship.
   b. the contrast effect.
   c. an assimilation effect.
   d. all of the above.

4. The most common form of cost-plus pricing is straight mark-up pricing, which: *(p.351)*
   a. is based on the costs involved in producing the product.
   b. occurs when price is calculated by adding a set percentage to the cost.
   c. calculates price by looking at both costs and what can be done to assure that a plant can operate at its capacity.
   d. subtracts a percentage of the cost from the cost to determine the selling price.

5. A method for setting prices which starts with a customer-pleasing price; the firm uses creative cost-management strategies in order to produce the product at a cost which will allow the firm to sell the product at that price is called: *(p.353)*
   a. price-floor pricing.
   b. demand pricing.
   c. chain-markup pricing.
   d. demand-backward pricing.

6. The parity pricing structure sets prices relative to the: *(p.354)*
   a. price leader.
   b. variable price.
   c. fixed price.
   d. markup price.

7. A pricing strategy in which a firm sets prices that provide ultimate value to customers is: *(p.355)*
   a. limit pricing.
   b. value pricing or every day low pricing (EDLP).
   c. negotiated pricing.
   d. reference pricing.

8. A strategy in which a firm charges a very high premium price for its new, highly desirable product is called: *(p.356)*
   a. dumping.
   b. penetration pricing.
   c. skimming pricing.
   d. pioneering pricing.

9. Pricing a new product low for a limited period of time in order to lower the risk for a customer is called: *(p.357)*
   a. limit pricing.
   b. penetration pricing.
   c. acceptance pricing.
   d. trial pricing.

10. An advertiser purchasing space in a group of magazines at a total package price is an example of: *(p.359)*
    a. captive pricing.
    b. price banding.
    c. price bundling.
    d. group pricing.

11. Seasonal discounts are: *(p.362)*
    a. price reductions offered only during certain times of the year.
    b. enticements to customers to pay their bills by the end of the season.
    c. options for customers to put seasonal items on lay-away.
    d. strategies to make customers accept shipment of a product by the end of the season.

12. The practice of charging different amounts for products, depending on how far they must be shipped, is called: *(p.359)*
    a. regional pricing.
    b. geographic pricing.
    c. distance pricing.
    d. delivery pricing.

13. F.O.B. factory means that: *(p.359)*
    a. the supplier will pay to have the product loaded onto a truck or some other carrier.
    b. both the cost of loading and transporting to the customer is included in the selling price and will be paid by the manufacturer.
    c. the cost of transportation is the responsibility of the factory.
    d. the cost of transporting the product from the factory to the customer's location is the responsibility of the customer.

14. Uniform delivered pricing means: *(p.360)*
    a. distant customers pay more while customers who are close to the factory pay less for the product.
    b. the seller absorbs the total cost of transportation.
    c. adding an average shipping cost to price.
    d. none of the above.

15. When the seller absorbs the total cost of transportation, this is known as: *(p.360)*
    a. freight absorption pricing.
    b. zone pricing.
    c. base-location pricing.
    d. designated pricing.

CHAPTER IN REVIEW—WRITING TO LEARN

1.   Discuss pricing objectives typically used in planning pricing strategies.

_____

_____

_____

_____

2.   Explain pricing tactics for individual and multiple products.

_____

_____

_____

_____

3.   Describe the pricing strategies discussed that are based upon the competition.

_____

_____

_____

CASE ANALYSIS

Real People, Real Decisions: Stephen Webb, Clarion Hotels Grand Pacific

Reread the three sections comprising the Clarion Hotels vignette in Chapter 13 and answer the following questions:

1.   How come operating costs at the two hotels were lower than if they had been separate hotels?

2.   How does price bundling apply to the hotel industry?

3.   What evidence suggests that Stephen Webb is using a price lining strategy in his hotels?

4.   Which new product pricing strategy might Stephen Webb use once his new addition is ready?

SCENARIO

You are the Product Manager of a new product—the first company to offer a detergent in "tablet" form—one tablet is used per wash. Results from the test market indicate that consumers find the tablets more convenient to use and not as messy as powder or liquid detergent. You are now faced with the challenge of pricing this new product for the broader market. Your company currently markets a powdered detergent, which can handle 50 washes, for $4.99 per box. It also markets a liquid detergent, which can handle 40 washes, for $6.29 per bottle. Your initial recommendation is to price the new product at 50 tablets for $6.99.

1.   Which psychological pricing strategy is evident in the pricing of all three products?
2.   Are you recommending a skimming or penetration pricing strategy? Why?
3.   Should trial pricing be considered in this situation? Why or why not?
4.   Would consumers have an internal reference price for this product? Why or why not?

ANSWERS

Chapter Outline

I.   PRICE PLANNING: MOVE AND COUNTERMOVE—How companies develop and manage pricing strategies, and some of the specific tactics that put pricing strategies in action.

II.   PRICING STRATEGIES—Can be based on costs, demand, the competition, and customer needs—as well as strategies for new products.

       A.   Pricing Strategies Based on Cost—Marketers use cost-based strategies because they are simple to calculate and relatively safe.

             1.   Cost-Plus Pricing—Method of setting prices in which the seller totals all the costs for the product and then adds the desired profit per unit.

             2.   Price-Floor Pricing—A method for calculating price in which, to maintain full plant operating capacity, a portion of a firm's output may be sold at a price that only covers marginal costs of production.

       B.   Pricing Strategies Based on Demand—A price-setting method based on estimates of demand at different prices.

             1.   Demand-Backward Pricing—Starts with a customer-pleasing price followed up with cost-management strategies to hold costs to a satisfactory level.

             2.   Chain-Markup Pricing—A pricing strategy that extends demand-backward pricing from the ultimate consumer all the way back through the channel of distribution to the manufacturer.

       C.   Pricing Strategies Based on the Competition
           Price Leader—The firm that sets price first in an industry; other major firms in an industry follow the leader by staying in line.

       D.   Pricing Strategies Based on Customers' Needs
           Value Pricing, or Every Day Low Pricing (EDLP)—A pricing strategy in which a firm sets prices which provide ultimate value to customers.

       E.   New Product Pricing

             1.   Skimming Price—A very high, premium price that a firm charges for its new, highly desirable product.

             2.   Penetration Pricing—A pricing strategy in which a new product is introduced at a very low price to encourage more customers to purchase it.

             3.   Trial Pricing—Pricing a new product low for a limited period of time in order to lower the risk for a customer.

III.   DEVELOPING PRICING TACTICS

       A.   Pricing For Individual Products

             1.   Two Part Pricing—Two separate types of payments are required to purchase the product.

             2.   Payment Pricing—Breaking up the total price into smaller amounts payable over time.

       B.   Pricing for Multiple Products
           Price Bundling—Selling two or more goods or services as a single package for one price.
           Captive Pricing—A pricing tactic for two items that must be used together; one item is priced very low and the firm makes its profit on another, high-margin item essential to the operation of the first item.

    C.   Geographic Pricing
        1.   F.O.B. Pricing

               F.O.B. Origin Pricing—A pricing tactic in which the cost of transporting the product from the factory to the customer's location is the responsibility of the customer.

               F.O.B. Delivered Pricing—A pricing tactic in which the cost of loading and transporting to the customer is included in the selling price and will be paid by the manufacturer.

        2.   Zone Pricing—A pricing tactic in which customers in different geographic zones pay different transportation rates.

        3.   Uniform Delivered Pricing—A pricing tactic in which a standard shipping charge is added to the price for all customers regardless of the distance from the seller.

        4.   Freight Absorption Pricing—A tactic where the seller absorbs the cost of transportation.

    D.   Discounting For Members of the Channel
        1.   Trade or Functional Discounts

               List Price—The price the end customer is expected to pay as determined by the manufacturer.

               Trade or Functional Discounts—Discounts off list price of products to members of the channel of distribution that perform various marketing functions.

        2.   Quantity Discounts—A pricing tactic of charging reduced prices for purchases of larger quantities of a product.

               Cumulative Quantity Discounts—Discounts based on the quantity bought within a specified time period.

               Noncumulative Quantity Discounts—Discounts based only on the quantity purchased with individual orders.

        3.   Cash Discounts—Incentives offered by firms to entice customers to pay their bills quickly.

        4.   Seasonal Discounts—Price reductions offered only during certain times of the year.

    E.   Pricing With Electronic Commerce—Technology is creating a pricing revolution.

IV.   PSYCHOLOGICAL ISSUES IN PRICING
    A.   Buyers' Pricing Expectations
        1.   Internal Reference Prices—A set or a price range in consumers' minds that they refer to in evaluating a product's price.

        2.   Price-Quality Inferences—When consumers use price as a cue or an indicator for quality.

    B.   Psychological Pricing Strategies
        1.   Odd-Even Pricing—Marketers have assumed that there is a psychological response to odd prices that differs from the response to even prices.

        2.   Price Lining—The practice of setting a limited number of different specific prices, called price points, for items in a product line.

V.   LEGAL AND ETHICAL CONSIDERATIONS IN PRICING
    A.   Deceptive Pricing Practices

        Bait-And-Switch—An illegal marketing practice in which an advertised price special is used as bait to get customers into the store with the intention of switching them to a higher-priced item.

    B.   Competition Act

        Predatory Pricing—Selling products at unreasonably low prices to drive a rival out of the market.

    C.   Price Discrimination—The Competition Act prohibits price discrimination—the illegal practice of offering the same product to different business customers at different prices and thus lessening competition.

    D.   Price Maintenance and Fixing—The collaboration of two or more firms in setting prices, usually to keep prices high.

        1.   Horizontal Price Fixing—When competitors making the same product jointly determine what price they will charge.

        2.   Vertical Price Fixing—When manufacturers or wholesalers attempt to force retailers to charge a certain price for their product.

Key Terms

1. Skimming price
2. Trial pricing
3. Cost-plus pricing
4. Price-floor pricing
5. Demand-based pricing
6. Chain-markup pricing
7. Price leader
8. Zone pricing
9. Parity pricing
10. Cumulative quantity discounts
11. Penetration pricing
12. Price bundling
13. Captive pricing
14. List price
15. Quantity discounts

Multiple Choice

1. b
2. a
3. c
4. b
5. d
6. a
7. b
8. c
9. d
10. c
11. a
12. b
13. d
14. c
15. a

Chapter in Review—Writing To Learn

1. Effective pricing objectives are designed to support corporate and marketing objectives and are flexible. Pricing objectives often focus on sales (e.g., to maximize sales or to increase market share) or may specify a desired level of profit growth or profit margin. At other times, firms may develop pricing strategies designed to pre-empt the competition or to increase customer satisfaction.

2. To implement pricing strategies with individual products, marketers may use two-part pricing or payment pricing tactics. For multiple products, marketers may use price bundling, wherein two or more products are sold and priced as a single package. Captive pricing is often chosen when two items must be used together; one item is sold at a very low price and the other at a high, profitable price.

3. Strategies based on the competition may represent industry wisdom but can be tricky due to the responses of competitive firms. A price leader strategy is often used in an oligopoly where it is best for all to avoid competition. A parity pricing strategy means that a firm sets the same price as competitors. Limit pricing occurs when a firm sets a low price for a new product in order to discourage new competitors.

Case Analysis

1. The two hotels share facilities, such as the athletic club and swimming pool, and make efficient use of shared services, including laundry, cleaning and external services. This helps reduce operating costs.

2. The customer is paying for a number of different services: use of the room, the housekeeping, room service availability, and the recreational facilities. The cost for all of these services is bundled in the room price.

3. Mr. Webb had different price points for each of his two hotels.

4. Mr. Webb could consider trial pricing, to encourage customers to stay in the new addition.

CHAPTER 14

Channel Management, Wholesaling, and Physical Distribution: Delivering the Product

CHAPTER OVERVIEW

The main purpose of this chapter is to explain what a distribution channel is and describe its functions in the marketing mix. A distribution channel is an organized network of firms that work together to get a product from a producer to a customer. Channels provide time, place and ownership utility for customers.

Manufacturer-owned channel members include sales branches, sales offices, and manufacturers' showrooms. Merchant wholesalers and merchandise agents and brokers are examples of independent intermediaries. Consumer distribution channels include direct distribution where the producer sells directly to consumers and indirect channels that may include a wholesaler and/or a retailer. Business-to-business channels are often direct, but may include industrial distributors, jobbers or dealers.

We next discussed the different types of decisions that must be made in distribution planning. Distribution planning begins with developing objectives that often relate to the level of market penetration. Next, marketers must consider environmental factors such as the characteristics of the product, existing channel relationships, intermediary availability, the number and density of customers, customer needs, and the distribution channels of competitors before they select the type of channel and the number of channel members. Vertical marketing systems are channels in which there is cooperation at the different levels. Horizontal marketing systems are composed of firms at one channel level who work together.

Lastly, we explored the types of decisions made in physical distribution planning. Physical distribution involves moving goods from the manufacturer to the customer in, hopefully, the most efficient and effective manner possible. Physical distribution includes sorting and grading of goods, order processing, materials handling, warehousing, transportation, and inventory control.

CHAPTER OBJECTIVES

1.   Explain what a distribution channel is and what functions distribution channels perform.

2.   Describe some of the types of wholesaling intermediaries found in distribution channels.

3.   Discuss the steps in planning distribution channel strategies.

4.   Describe the activities that are important in the physical distribution of goods.

5.   Discuss the distribution implications of the Internet.

CHAPTER OUTLINE

With reference to the textbook, please provide a brief description of each of the main elements listed in the Chapter Outline below. The page numbers will help guide you through the learning process.

I.   PLACE: THE FINAL FRONTIER _____ *(p.380)*

II.   THE IMPORTANCE OF DISTRIBUTION: YOU CAN'T SELL
      WHAT ISN'T THERE!
      A.   What is a Distribution Channel? _____ *(p.381)*
            Channel Intermediaries _____ *(p.381)*
      B.   Functions of Distribution Channels _____ *(p.381)*
            Bulk Breaking _____ *(p.382)*
            Creating Assortments _____ *(p.382)*
            Facilitating Functions _____ *(p.383)*

III. THE COMPOSITION AND STRUCTURE OF CHANNELS
      A.   Types of Wholesaling Intermediaries _____ *(p.383)*
            1.   Independent Intermediaries _____ *(p.383)*
                  Merchant Wholesalers_____ *(p.383)*
                  Take Title _____ *(p.383)*
                  a.   Full-Service Merchant Wholesaler _____ *(p.383)*
                        Rack Jobber _____ *(p.384)*
                  b.   Limited-Service Merchant Wholesaler ___ *(p.384)*
                        Cash-and-Carry Wholesalers _____ *(p.384)*
                        Truck Jobbers _____ *(p.384)*
                        Drop Shippers _____ *(p.384)*
                        Mail-Order Wholesalers _____ *(p.385)*
                        Merchandise Agents or Brokers _____ *(p.385)*
                        Manufacturers' Agents _____ *(p.385)*
                        Selling Agents_____ *(p.385)*
                        Commission Merchants _____ *(p.385)*
                        Merchandise Brokers _____ *(p.385)*
            2.   Manufacturer-Owned Intermediaries _____ *(p.386)*
                  Sales Branches _____ *(p.386)*
                  Sales Offices _____ *(p.386)*
                  Manufacturers' Showrooms _____ *(p.386)*

B.   Types of Distribution Channels _____ *(p.386)*
          Channel Levels _____ *(p.386)*
          1.   Consumer Channels _____ *(p.386)*
              Manufacturer-Retailer-Consumer Channel _____ *(p.388)*
              Manufacturer-Wholesaler-Retailer-Consumer
              Channel _____ *(p.388)*
          2.   Business-to-Business Channels _____ *(p.388)*
          3.   Distribution Channels for Services _____ *(p.389)*
          4.   Dual Distribution Systems _____ *(p.390)*

IV.   PLANNING A CHANNEL STRATEGY _____ *(p.390)*
      A.   Channel Objectives _____ *(p.390)*
      B.   Evaluating the Environment _____ *(p.390)*
      C.   Choosing a Distribution System _____ *(p.391)*
          1.   Conventional, Vertical, and Horizontal Systems
              Conventional Marketing System_____ *(p.391)*
              Vertical Marketing System _____ *(p.391)*
              Horizontal Marketing System _____ *(p.392)*
          2.   Intensive, Exclusive, and Selective Distribution
              Intensive Distribution _____ *(p.393)*
              Exclusive Distribution_____ *(p.393)*
              Selective Distribution _____ *(p.393)*
      D.   Developing Distribution Tactics _____ *(p.394)*
          1.   Selecting Channel Partners _____ *(p.394)*
               Managing the Channel of Distribution
              Channel Leader _____ *(p.395)*
      E.   Distribution Channels and the Marketing Mix _____ *(p.395)*

V.   PHYSICAL DISTRIBUTION
      A.   What is Physical Distribution? _____ *(p.396)*
          1.   Order Processing_____ *(p.396)*
          2.   Warehousing _____ *(p.397)*
          3.   Materials Handling _____ *(p.397)*
          4.   Transportation _____ *(p.398)*
          5.   Inventory Control _____ *(p.399)*

KEY TERMS

Select the correct term for each definition and write it in the space provided.

Direct channel
Horizontal marketing system
Channel levels
Warehousing
Merchant wholesaler
Bulk breaking
Indirect distribution
Channel leader

Merchandise handling
Channel of distribution
Intensive distribution
Conventional marketing system
Vertical marketing system (VMS)
Creating assortments
Exclusive distribution

1. _____ The series of firms or individuals that work together to get a product from the producer to the final consumer. *(p.381)*

2. _____ Intermediaries that buy goods from manufacturers (i.e., take title to them) and sell to other retailers and other business-to-business customers. *(p.383)*

3. _____ The number of distinct categories of intermediaries who populate a channel of distribution. *(p.386)*

4. _____ A channel of distribution in which there are no intermediaries or middle levels. *(p.381)*

5. _____ Distribution of goods in which manufacturers reach end-users through intermediaries—wholesalers, dealers, distributors, agents and/or retailers. *(p.381)*

6. _____ Providing a variety of products in one location to meet the needs of buyers. *(p.382)*

7. _____ A multiple-level distribution channel in which channel members work independently of one another. *(p.391)*

8. _____ A channel of distribution in which there is cooperation among members of the manufacturing, wholesaling, and retailing levels. *(p.391)*

9. _____ The moving of products into, within, and out of warehouses. *(p.397)*

10. _____ An arrangement within a channel of distribution in which two or more firms at the same channel level work together for a common purpose. *(p.392)*

11. _____ Selling a product through all suitable wholesalers or retailers who are willing to stock and sell the product. *(p.393)*

12. _____ Selling a product only through a single outlet in a particular region. *(p.393)*

13. _____ A firm at one level of distribution that takes a leadership role, establishing operating norms and processes that reduce channel conflicts, reduce costs, and enhance delivered customer value. *(p.395)*

14. _____ Storing goods in anticipation of sale or transfer to another member of the channel of distribution. *(p.397)*

15. _____ Dividing larger quantities of goods into smaller lots in order to meet the needs of buyers. *(p.382)*

MULTIPLE CHOICE

Identify the most correct answer.

1. Effective channels of distribution provide the following physical distribution function(s): *(p.382)*
   a. Breaking bulk.
   b. Creating assortments.
   c. Reducing transactions.
   d. All of the above.

2. Sales branches are: *(p.386)*
   a. wholesaler-type facilities owned and run by a manufacturer.
   b. typically located in strategic geographic areas in order to be closer to customers and there are no inventories.
   c. producer-owned facilities where customers visit to examine the firm's products attractively displayed.
   d. set up by manufacturers only in order to reduce selling costs.

3. Full-service merchant wholesalers who regularly call on retailers are: *(p.384)*
   a. general-merchandise wholesalers.
   b. limited-line wholesalers.
   c. rack jobbers.
   d. drop shippers.

4. Manufacturers' agents: *(p.385)*
   a. handle the entire product line of one or more producers.
   b. are independent salespeople who carry several product lines of noncompeting manufacturers.
   c. assist in the sale of products by identifying likely buyers and sellers, bringing them together, and helping them make a purchase agreement.
   d. typically are found in agricultural markets such as grain, livestock, and produce.

5. Export/import intermediaries that facilitate transactions in markets such as real estate, food, and used equipment are known as: *(p.385)*
   a. commission merchants.
   b. sales agents.
   c. merchandise brokers.
   d. sales brokers.

6. Reason(s) why some manufacturers decide to sell directly to their customers rather than delegating this task to channel intermediaries include: *(p.386)*
   a. There are some instances where the direct channel allows the customer to be better served at a lower cost.
   b. When the producer handles distribution, it maintains control of pricing, service, delivery—all of the elements of the transaction.
   c. Direct distribution is sometimes the only way to gain customer interest in a new product.
   d. All of the above.

7. Business-to-business distribution channels are: *(p.388)*
   a. networks designed to facilitate the flow of goods from a producer to an organizational or business customer.
   b. the most common form of distribution channels in consumer markets.
   c. frequently used when products are distributed through very large retailers.
   d. more frequently indirect channels than in consumer markets.

8.   If the product is being distributed through more than one type of channel, this is called: *(p.390)*
       a.   vertical distribution.
       b.   disorganized distribution.
       c.   dual or multiple distribution.
       d.   horizontal distribution.

9.   Not only do marketers need to consider who is buying and why they are buying, but they must also know: *(p.390)*
       a.   whether customers want large or small quantities.
       b.   whether customers will buy from a distant supplier.
       c.   how long customers are willing to wait for their purchases.
       d.   all of the above.

10.   In an administered VMS: *(p.391)*
       a.   cooperation among members at the manufacturing, wholesaling, and retailing levels is legally enforced.
       b.   voluntary cooperation is enforced by a channel leader.
       c.   independent firms sign contracts that spell out how they will cooperate.
       d.   retail members of a chain typically use a common name, cooperate in advertising and other promotions, and even develop their own private-label products.

11.   Types of contractual VMSs include: *(p.391)*
       a.   wholesaler-sponsored voluntary chains.
       b.   retailer cooperatives.
       c.   franchises.
       d.   all of the above.

12.   Distribution using fewer outlets than in intensive distribution but more than in exclusive distribution is called: *(p.393)*
       a.   selective distribution.
       b.   independent distribution.
       c.   conventional distribution.
       d.   midpoint distribution.

13.   The ability of the carrier to deliver goods, safely and on time is referred to as: *(p.398)*
       a.   speed of delivery.
       b.   dependability.
       c.   capability.
       d.   accessibility.

14.   A process, developed to insure that the types and quantities of goods needed to meet customers' demands are always available, is called: *(p.399)*
       a.   materials handling.
       b.   order processing.
       c.   inventory control.
       d.   trade loading.

15.   The focus on managing the logistics of one's entire supply chain is known as: *(p.400)*
       a.   Just In Time Delivery.
       b.   supply chain management.
       c.   inventory control management.
       d.   electronic data interchange (EDI).

CHAPTER IN REVIEW—WRITING TO LEARN

1.   Explain what a distribution channel is and describe its functions in the marketing mix.

_____

_____

_____

_____

2.   Describe the characteristics of vertical marketing systems (VMSs).

_____

_____

_____

_____

3.   Identify the primary activities that are involved in physical distribution.

_____

_____

_____

_____

CASE ANALYSIS

Real People, Real Decisions: Ryan Hobenshield, HARTMANN Group

Reread the three sections comprising the HARTMANN vignette in Chapter 14 and answer the following questions:

1. What type of wholesaling intermediary is Hobenshield considering in Option 1, and what are the major advantages of this type of intermediary?

2. Why might the five current Australian partners have been reluctant to develop HARTMANN's consumer channel? In thinking about your answer, reflect on what you learned in Chapters 6 and 7 about the differences between consumer and business buying practices.

3. Identify the channel structure HARTMANN is considering in Option 3 for the distribution of consumer products in Australia.

4. What implicit criteria is HARTMANN using to assess its distribution options?

SCENARIO

Your friend completed her certificate in Fashion Design last spring, and has since been working steadily on the development of her own line of women's clothing. She now needs marketing help, and has come to you for advice on the best way to get her wares distributed in Canada.

1. Which business-to-business channels might she consider using to distribute her clothing line?
2. Which business-to-consumer channels might she consider using to distribute her clothing line?
3. Discuss the advantages and disadvantages of using a *direct* channel to distribute her clothing line.
4. Which distribution intensity would be most achievable for a clothing line designed by a recent Fashion Design graduate—intensive, selective or exclusive?

ANSWERS

Chapter Outline

I.   PLACE: THE FINAL FRONTIER—Making goods and services available where and when customers need and want them.

II.   THE IMPORTANCE OF DISTRIBUTION: YOU CAN'T SELL WHAT ISN'T THERE!
    A.   What is a Distribution Channel?—A series of firms or individuals that facilitates the movement of a product from a producer to the final customer.
            Channel Intermediaries—Firms or individuals such as wholesalers, agents, brokers, or retailers who help move a product from the producer to the consumer or business user.
    B.   Functions of Distribution Channels—Channels provide time, place, and ownership utility for customers. In addition, channels increase the efficiency of the flow of goods from producer to consumer.
            Bulk Breaking—Dividing larger quantities of goods into smaller lots in order to meet the needs of buyers.
            Creating Assortments—Providing a variety of products in one location to meet the needs of buyers.
            Facilitating Functions—Functions of channel intermediaries that make the purchase process easier for customers and manufacturers.

III.   THE COMPOSITION AND STRUCTURE OF CHANNELS
    A.   Types of Wholesaling Intermediaries—Firms that handle the flow of products from the manufacturer to the retailer or business user.
            1.   Independent Intermediaries—Channel intermediaries that are not controlled by any manufacturer but instead do business with many different manufacturers and many different customers.
                    Merchant Wholesalers—Intermediaries that buy goods from manufacturers (take title to them) and sell to retailers and other business-to-business customers.
                    Take Title—To accept legal ownership of a product and the accompanying rights and responsibilities of ownership.
                    a.   Full-Service Merchant Wholesaler—Provide a wide range of services for their customers (delivery, credit, etc.).
                            Rack Jobber—Supplies retailers with specialty items.
                    b.   Limited-Service Merchant Wholesaler—Provide fewer services for their customers.
                            Cash-and-carry wholesalers—Provide low-cost merchandise for retailers and industrial customers who are too small for other wholesalers' sales representatives to call on them.
                            Truck Jobbers—Carry their products to small business customer locations for their inspection and selection.
                            Drop shippers—Limited function wholesalers that take title to the merchandise but never actually take possession of it.
                            Mail-order wholesalers—Sell products to small retailers and other industrial customers, through catalogues.
                    Merchandise Agents or Brokers—Channel intermediaries that provide services in exchange for commissions but never take title to the product.
                    Manufacturers' Agents—(Manufacturers' reps), are independent salespeople who carry several lines of noncompeting products.
                    Selling Agents—(Including export/import agents) market a whole product line or one manufacturer's total output.

Commission Merchants—Sales agents who receive goods, on consignment, while taking possession of the products without taking title.

Merchandise Brokers—Identify likely buyers and sellers and bring the two together in return for a fee received.

2.   Manufacturer-Owned Intermediaries—Separate business units that perform all of the functions of independent intermediaries, while maintaining complete control over the channel.

Sales Branches—Manufacturer-owned facilities that carry inventory and provide sales and service to customers in a specific geographic area.

Sales Offices—Like agents, they do not carry inventory but provide selling functions for the manufacturer in a specific geographic area.

Manufacturers' Showrooms—Facilities in which products are permanently displayed for customers to visit.

B.   Types of Distribution Channels—Marketing manager must select a channel structure that creates a competitive advantage for the firm and its products based on the size and needs of the target market.

Channel Levels—The number of distinct categories of intermediaries that populate the channel of distribution.

1.   Consumer Channels—The simplest channel is a direct channel, (the manufacturer sells directly to customers).

Manufacturer-Retailer-Consumer Channel.

Manufacturer-Wholesaler-Retailer-Consumer Channel.

2.   Business-to-Business Channels—Direct channels are more common here than in consumer markets.

3.   Distribution Channels For Services—Most services travel directly from the producer to the consumer.

4.   Dual or Multiple Distribution Systems—When manufacturers, dealers, wholesalers, retailers, and customers interact with more than one type of channel.

IV.   PLANNING A CHANNEL STRATEGY—A focus on the distribution planning of producers or manufacturers because of the leadership role accepted in creating a successful distribution channel.

A.   Channel Objectives—Develop appropriate objectives that support the organization's overall marketing goals.

B.   Evaluating the Environment—Marketers must consider their internal and external environments.

C.   Choosing a Distribution System—Three basic decisions that must be made are: the number of levels in the distribution channel, channel relationships, and the distribution intensity.

1.   Conventional, Vertical, and Horizontal Marketing Systems

Conventional Marketing System—A multiple-level distribution channel in which channel members work independently of one another.

Vertical Marketing System—A channel of distribution in which there is cooperation among members at the manufacturing, wholesaling, and retailing levels.

Horizontal Marketing System—An arrangement within a channel of distribution in which two or more firms at the same channel level work together for a common purpose.

2.   Intensive, Exclusive, and Selective Distribution

Intensive Distribution—Selling a product through all suitable wholesalers or retailers that are willing to stock and sell the product.

Exclusive Distribution—Selling a product only through a single outlet in a particular region.

Selective Distribution—Distribution using fewer outlets than in intensive distribution but more than in exclusive distribution.

D.   Developing Distribution Tactics—Decisions concerning the type of distribution system to use such as a direct or indirect channel, or a conventional or an integrated channel.
  1.   Selecting Channel Partners—The channel relationship may be affected by the contribution level of each member concerning profit, service, and control.
  2.   Managing the Channel of Distribution
       Channel Leader—A firm at one level of distribution that takes a leadership role, establishing operating norms and processes that reduce channel conflicts, reduce costs, and enhance delivered customer value.
E.   Distribution Channels and the Marketing Mix—Place decisions affect pricing.

V.   PHYSICAL DISTRIBUTION
  A.   What is Physical Distribution?—The activities used to move finished goods from manufacturers to final customers including order processing, warehousing, materials handling, transportation, and inventory control.
    1.   Order Processing—The activities that occur between the time an order is received and shipped.
    2.   Warehousing—Storing goods in anticipation of sale or transfer to another member of the channel of distribution.
    3.   Materials Handling—The moving of products into, within, and out of warehouses.
    4.   Transportation—The modes of transportation include railroads, pipelines, water transportation, motor carriers, and airways, each differing in dependability, cost, speed of delivery, accessibility, capability and traceability.
    5.   Inventory Control—Activities to ensure that goods are always available to meet customers' demands.

Key Terms

1.	Channel of distribution	
2.	Merchant wholesalers	
3.	Channel levels	
4.	Direct channel	
5.	Indirect distribution	
6.	Creating assortments	
7.	Conventional marketing system	
8.	Vertical marketing system (VMS)	
9.	Merchandise handling	
10.	Horizontal marketing system	
11.	Intensive distribution	
12.	Exclusive distribution	
13.	Channel leader	
14.	Warehousing	
15.	Breaking bulk	

Multiple Choice

1.	d
2.	a
3.	c
4.	b
5.	c
6.	d
7.	a
8.	c
9.	d
10.	b
11.	d
12.	a
13.	b
14.	c
15.	b

Chapter in Review—Writing To Learn

1. A distribution channel is an organized network of firms that work together to get a product from a producer to a customer. Channels provide time, place and ownership utility for customers. Channel members handle the physical distribution function for products including the breaking and accumulation of bulk, creating assortments, reducing the number of transactions necessary for the flow of goods, transportation and storage. Intermediaries in channels of distribution also perform a variety of both communications and facilitating functions.

2. Vertical marketing systems (VMSs) are channels in which there is cooperation at the different levels. VMSs include administered and contractual VMSs, wholesaler sponsored voluntary chains, retailer cooperatives, franchises and corporate VMSs.

3. Physical distribution involves moving goods from the manufacturer to the customer in, hopefully, the most efficient and effective manner possible. Physical distribution includes sorting and grading of goods, order processing, materials handling, warehousing, transportation, and inventory control.

Case Analysis

1. In Option 1, HARTMANN is considering setting up a sales office in Australia. The main advantages of this type of intermediary are: a) control over the pace and approach to market development b) inventory control (no more global inventory crises!) and c) capitalizing on the sales group's knowledge of local market requirements.

2. The five existing Australian partners have developed expertise in business-to-business marketing – nurturing relationships with professional buyers, negotiating terms, attending trade shows, and dealing with existing and prospective clients one-on-one. Developing the consumer channel requires expertise in marketing to the masses: developing a branding strategy, launching an advertising campaign, creating consumer promotions, etc. Their poor performance during the trial period suggests that while the existing Australian partners had considerable expertise in business-to-business marketing, they did not have the consumer marketing skills required to be successful.

3. The channel structure HARTMANN is considering for the distribution of its consumer products in Australia is Manufacturer-Wholesaler-Retailer-Consumer.

4. In considering the pros and cons of each option, Hobenshield's implicit criteria are: speed to market and degree of control over the channel.

CHAPTER 15

Retailing and E-Tailing

CHAPTER OVERVIEW

We began this chapter by explaining the position of retailing in the marketplace. Any person or organization that offers something for sale to a consumer is a retailer. The wheel of retailing hypothesis suggests that new retailers compete on price and then move upscale leaving room for other new low-price entrants. The retail life cycle theory suggests retailing institutions are introduced, grow, reach maturity, and then decline.

We learned about some of the environmental changes which will have an impact on the future of retailing as represented in demographic changes, technological developments, environmentally conscious consumers, and market globalization.

Retailers are classified by the merchandise assortment carried, and the different types include: convenience stores, supermarkets, specialty stores, discount stores, off price retailers, warehouse clubs, department stores, and hypermarkets. In developing a retailing strategy, marketers seek to develop a desirable store image which includes atmospherics, store personnel, pricing policy, and store location.

E-tailing is the concept of selling goods directly to consumers over the Internet. We looked at who shops online, why they do so, and what they buy. We learned about bots, push technology and portals, and examined some of the critical success factors and barriers to success in e-tailing. We also looked at other forms of nonstore retailing, which included traditional mail-order shopping, direct selling operations, and vending machines as well as newer forms of direct marketing such home shopping networks and telemarketing.

CHAPTER OBJECTIVES

1.   Define retailing and describe how retailing has evolved over time.

2.   Classify retailers by their selection of merchandise.

3.   Understand the importance of store image to a retail positioning strategy and explain some of the actions a retailer can take to create a desired image in the marketplace.

4.   Describe the opportunities and barriers to e-tailing.

5.   Describe the major forms of nonstore retailing.

CHAPTER OUTLINE

With reference to the textbook, please provide a brief description of each of the main elements listed in the Chapter Outline below. The page numbers will help guide you through the learning process.

I.   RETAILING: SPECIAL DELIVERY _____ *(p.408)*
     A.   Retailing: A Mixed (Shopping) Bag _____ *(p.408)*
     B.   The Evolution of Retailing
          1.   The Wheel of Retailing (Hypothesis) _____ *(p.409)*
          2.   The Retail Life-Cycle _____ *(p.409)*
     C.   The Evolution Continues: What's "In Store"
     For the Future _____ *(p.410)*
          1.   Demographics _____ *(p.410)*
          2.   Technology _____ *(p.411)*
          3.   Globalization _____ *(p.411)*

II.   TYPES OF RETAILERS
     A.   Classifying Retailers by What They Sell_____ *(p.412)*
          1.   Merchandise Assortment_____ *(p.413)*
          2.   Merchandise Breadth _____ *(p.413)*
          3.   Merchandise Depth _____ *(p.413)*
          4.   Scrambled Merchandising_____ *(p.413)*
          5.   Inventory Turnover _____ *(p.413)*
     B.   Classifying Retailers by the Selection of Merchandise
     They Sell
          1.   Convenience Stores_____ *(p.414)*
          2.   Supermarkets_____ *(p.414)*
          3.   Specialty Stores_____ *(p.414)*
          4.   Discount Stores _____ *(p.414)*
               Off-Price Retailers_____ *(p.414)*
               Warehouse Clubs _____ *(p.414)*
          5.   Department Stores_____ *(p.414)*
          6.   Hypermarkets _____ *(p.415)*

III.   DEVELOPING A STORE POSITIONING STRATEGY:
     RETAILING AS THEATRE
     A.   Store Image _____ *(p.416)*
          Atmospherics_____ *(p.417)*
          1.   Store Design: Setting the Stage_____ *(p.417)*
          2.   The Actors: Store Personne_____ *(p.419)*
          3.   Pricing Policy: How Much for a Ticket to the Show? *(p.419)*
     B.   Building the Theatre: Store Location
     Types of Store Locations_____ *(p.420)*
          1.   Site Selection: Choosing Where to Build _____ *(p.420)*

IV.   E-TAILING AND OTHER NON-STORE RETAILING
    A.   E-Tailing _____ *(p.422)*
            Who Shops Online? _____ *(p.423)*
            Why Do They Shop Online? _____ *(p.424)*
            1.   Bots _____ *(p.424)*
            2.   Push Technology _____ *(p.425)*
            3.   Portals _____ *(p.425)*
            What Do They Buy? _____ *(p.425)*
            Critical Success Factors _____ *(p.427)*
            Scalability _____ *(p.428)*
            Barriers to Success _____ *(p.428)*
    B.   Direct Marketing _____ *(p.427)*
            1.   Mail Order _____ *(p.427)*
            2.   Catalogues _____ *(p.427)*
            3.   Direct Mail _____ *(p.428)*
    C.   Direct Selling _____ *(p.428)*
            1.   Door-to-Door Sales _____ *(p.428)*
            2.   Parties and Networks _____ *(p.428)*
            3.   Telemarketing _____ *(p.429)*
    D.   Automatic Vending _____ *(p.429)*
    E.   Direct-Response Television _____ *(p.429)*
            1.   Infomercials _____ *(p.430)*
            2.   Home Shopping Networks _____ *(p.430)*

KEY TERMS

Select the correct term for each definition and write it in the space provided.

Hypermarkets   Retail life cycle
Merchandise breadth   Direct marketing
E-tailing   Traffic flow
Wheel of retailing hypothesis   Supermarkets
Specialty stores   General merchandise discount stores
Trade area   Merchandise depth
Inventory turnover   Store image
Non store retailing

1.   _____   A theory that explains how retail firms
                                        change, becoming more upscale as they go
                                        through their life cycle. *(p.409)*

2.   _____   A process that focuses on the various retail
                                        life cycle stages from introduction to decline.
                                        (p.409)

3. _____ The direction in which shoppers will move through the store and what areas they will pass or avoid. *(p.417)*

4. _____ The average number of times a year a retailer expects to sell its inventory. *(p.413)*

5. _____ The number of different product lines available. *(p.413)*

6. _____ The variety of choices available for each specific product. *(p.413)*

7. _____ Food stores that carry a wide selection of edibles and related products. *(p.414)*

8. _____ Retailers that carry only a few product lines but offer good selection within the lines they do sell. *(p.414)*

9. _____ Retailers that sell a broad range of items at low prices with minimal service. *(p.414)*

10. _____ Retailers with the characteristics of both warehouse stores and supermarkets; hypermarkets are several times larger than other stores and offer virtually everything from grocery items to electronics. *(p.415)*

11. _____ The way a retailer is perceived in the marketplace relative to the competition. *(p.417)*

12. _____ Any method used to complete an exchange with a product end-user that does not require a customer visit to a store. *(p.422)*

13. _____ Exposing a consumer to information about a good or service through a nonpersonal medium and convincing the customer to respond with an order. *(p.422)*

14. _____ Offering products for sale directly to consumers through the Internet. *(p.422)*

15. _____ A geographic zone that accounts for the majority of a store's sales and customers. *(p.421)*

MULTIPLE CHOICE

Identify the most correct answer.

1. In the introduction stage of the retail life cycle theory: *(p.409)*
   a. the concept of the business catches on and profits go up.
   b. market share stabilizes and profits decline.
   c. the new retailer often is an aggressive entrepreneur who takes a unique approach to doing business.
   d. the retail business becomes obsolete.

2. The range of products sold is known as: *(p.413)*
   a. merchandise assortment.
   b. merchandise breadth.
   c. merchandise depth.
   d. merchandise width.

3. Neighbourhood retailers that carry a limited number of frequently purchased items including basic food products, newspapers, and sundries and cater to consumers who are willing to pay a premium for the ease of buying close to home are: *(p.414)*
   a. supermarkets.
   b. convenience stores.
   c. specialty stores.
   d. discount stores.

4. Retailers who offer a wide variety of inexpensive brand name items at low prices with minimal service are: *(p.414)*
   a. off-price retailers.
   b. factory outlet stores.
   c. hypermarkets.
   d. general merchandise discount stores.

5. Off price retailers: *(p.414)*
   a. offer a broad assortment of items.
   b. feature the depth of assortment found in department stores.
   c. emphasize well-known brand names at high prices.
   d. none of the above.

6. The way a retailer is perceived in the marketplace relative to the competition is called: *(p.417)*
   a. store image.
   b. retailer acceptability.
   c. store design.
   d. retailer effectiveness.

7. The use of colour, lighting, scents, furniture, and other design elements to create a desired store image is: *(p.417)*
   a. store design.
   b. store layout.
   c. atmospherics.
   d. store definition.

8. The basic types of retail locations include: *(p.420)*
   a. business districts.
   b. shopping centres.
   c. freestanding retailers.
   d. all of the above.

9. A Central Business District (CBD): *(p.420)*
   a. refers to a smaller area with at least one department or variety store at a major intersection.
   b. is a shopping area where public transportation is usually available.
   c. evolves to satisfy convenience-oriented neighbourhood shopping needs.
   d. features a greater diversity of merchandise.

10. A store's trade area is affected by: *(p.426)*
    a. its proximity to a population centre.
    b. the number of anchor stores in the shopping district.
    c. the sharing of costs.
    d. the pricing of the merchandise.

11. A pure play e-tailer: *(p.423)*
    a. offers products for sale only via the Internet.
    b. has store locations in major malls.
    c. has store locations in major recreational centres.
    d. none of the above.

12. When a company representative makes a sales presentation to a group of people who have gathered in the home of a friend or acquaintance, and participants get caught up in the "group spirit" and buy things they would normally not if they had been on their own, this is known as: *(p.431)*
    a. a home shopping club.
    b. telemarketing.
    c. a party plan system.
    d. direct mail.

13. Door-to-door selling is declining markedly in North America due to: *(p.431)*
    a. women feeling richer when they are away from home.
    b. the large numbers of houses that are empty during the day due to the increase in working women.
    c. the increasing reluctance of those who are at home to admit strangers.
    d. all of the above.

14. Push technology refers to: *(p.425)*
    a. a program by the software companies to increase the number of electronic retailing Web sites.
    b. Internet tools that allow marketers to send information they think is relevant to consumers directly to their computers.
    c. the newest marketing campaign of a major Internet company to switch customers to their service.
    d. a computer virus that has invaded certain electronic catalogues.

15. Example(s) of barriers to success of electronic commerce include: *(p.428-429)*
    a. Shoppers receive instant gratification from electronic commerce.
    b. Customers readily provide sensitive data such as credit card numbers.
    c. People need "touch and feel" information before buying many products.
    d. all of the above.

CHAPTER IN REVIEW—WRITING TO LEARN

1. Describe how retailers may be classified by type or selection of merchandise.

    _____

    _____

    _____

    _____

2.   Identify and describe the major types of retail locations.

_____

_____

_____

_____

3.   What are two of the critical success factors involved in e-tailing?

_____

_____

_____

_____

CASE ANALYSIS

Real People, Real Decisions: Göran Carstedt, IKEA

Reread the three sections comprising the IKEA vignette in Chapter 15 and answer the following questions:

1.   Where is IKEA based and from where does the majority of its sales originate?

2.   What is IKEA's mission statement?

3.   Why was IKEA concerned about the entry of STR in the L.A. marketplace?

4.   What did IKEA consider when evaluating potential store sites?

SCENARIO

You and a friend are planning to open a juice bar on campus. You are only beginning to think about the many decisions you have to make. Here are a few questions to get you started:

1.   What type of merchandise assortment will you carry?
2.   Discuss the atmospherics of the juice bar. What might appeal to your target market of students, faculty and staff?
3.   What is your trade area?
4.   How do you plan to position your store's image, relative to your local competition, and in comparison to existing juice bars—what will make yours "different and better"?

ANSWERS

Chapter Outline

I.   RETAILING: SPECIAL DELIVERY—Retailing is the final stop in the distribution channel by which goods and services are sold to consumers for their personal use.

      A.   Retailing: A Mixed (Shopping) Bag—Part of what makes retailing such an exciting area is that the same good or service can be obtained in so many different ways.

      B.   The Evolution of Retailing

            1.   The Wheel of Retailing Hypothesis—A theory that explains how retail firms change, becoming more upscale as they go through their life cycle.

            2.   The Retail Life Cycle—A process that focuses on the various retail life cycle stages, from introduction to decline.

      C.   The Evolution Continues: What's "In Store" For the Future—Three important factors motivate innovative merchants to reinvent the way they do business.

            1.   Demographics—Retailers need to constantly refine their merchandise mix to meet the needs of a changing market.

                  a.   Working Women—The dramatic increase in the number of working women has made the problem of "time poverty" even more acute.

                  b.   Age Segmentation—Retailers are increasingly recognizing that consumers in different age groups vary dramatically in terms of what they look for in a retail environment.

                  c.   Ethnic Diversity—Although members of every ethnic group can usually find small, local retailers that understand and cater to their specific needs and subculture, larger operations must begin to tailor their strategies to the cultural makeup of specific trade areas.

            2.   Technology

                  a.   Technological Developments—Exciting new developments are constantly being introduced by retailers.

                         Point of Sale (POS) Systems—Retail computer systems that collect sales data and are hooked directly into the store's inventory control system.

            3.   Globalization

                  a.   Globalization is a two-way street—Innovative international retailing concepts are influencing Canadian retailing.

II.   TYPES OF RETAILERS

      A.   Classifying Retailers by What They Sell—One of the most important strategic decisions a retailer has to make is what to sell—its merchandise.

            1.   Merchandise Assortment—The range of products sold.

            2.   Merchandise Breadth—The number of different product lines available.

            3.   Merchandise Depth—The variety of choices available for each specific product.

            Scrambled Merchandising—carrying a mixture of items that are not directly related to each other.

            Inventory Turnover—The average number of times a year a retailer expects to sells its inventory.

      B.   Store Types

            1.   Convenience Stores—Neighbourhood retailers that carry a limited number of frequently purchased items including basic food products, newspapers, and sundries and cater to consumers who are willing to pay a premium for the ease of buying close to home.

            2.   Supermarkets—Food stores that carry a wide selection of edibles and related products.

            3.   Specialty Stores—Retailers who carry only a few product lines but offer good selection within the lines they do sell.

4.   Discount Stores—Retailers who offer a wide variety of inexpensive brand name items in a self-service, "no-frills" setting.

         Off-Price Retailers—Retailers who buy surplus merchandise from well-known manufacturers and pass the savings on to customers.

         Mass Merchandisers—Retailers who offer a very large assortment of items.

5.   Department Stores—Retailers who sell a broad range of items and a good selection within each product line sold.

6.   Hypermarkets—Retailers with the characteristics of both warehouse stores and supermarkets; hypermarkets are several times larger than other stores and offer virtually everything from grocery items to electronics.

III.   DEVELOPING A STORE POSITIONING STRATEGY: RETAILING AS THEATRE—Many retailers recognize the importance of using visual and other sensory cues to create a store environment that reflects and perpetuates a desired image.

     A.   Store Image—The way a retailer is perceived in the marketplace relative to the competition.

         Atmospherics—The use of colour, lighting, scents, furnishings, and other design elements to create a desired store image.

         1.   Store Design—Some specific design decisions include store layout, fixture type and merchandise density, sound type and density, and colour and lighting.

         2.   The Actors: Store Personnel—Store personnel should be carefully selected to complement a store's image.

         3.   Pricing Policy: How Much for a Ticket to the Show?—A store's pricing policy influences shoppers' perceptions of the "type" of store it is.

     B.   Building the Theatre: Store Location

         Types of Store Locations—There are four basic types of retail locations: A store can be found in a business district, in a shopping centre, as a free standing entity, or in a nontraditional location.

         1.   Site Selection: Choosing Where to Build—Store location is a key strategic decision that affects a company's ability to operate effectively, turnover, and store image. Location planners often try to determine if an area needs a new store in the first place—put simply, locations can be evaluated in terms of whether they are saturated, understored, or overstored.

IV.   E-TAILING AND OTHER NONSTORE RETAILING

     A.   E-tailing—Offering products for sale directly to consumers over the Internet.

         Nonstore Retailing—Any method used to complete an exchange with a product end-user that does not require a customer visit to a store.

         Who Shops Online?—Online shoppers are now, on average, older, increasingly female, less affluent and less highly educated than they once were.

         Why Do They Shop Online?—They shop online to achieve a variety of benefits, known as the six Cs; cost, choice, convenience, customization, communication and control.

         1.   Bots—Electronic robots or shopping agents that help consumers find products and prices on the Internet.

         2.   Push Technology—Internet tools that allow marketers to send information they think is relevant to consumers directly to their computers.

         3.   Portals—Gateways to the Internet that assists consumers to navigate the Internet and customize their experience.

         What Do They Buy?—Travel services, computer hardware and software, financial services and collectibles represented over 70% of North American e-tail sales in 1999.

         Critical Success Factors—Branding and customer loyalty are critical success factors in e-tailing.

         Scalability—The ability of organizations to get bigger without a big rise in expenses.

         Barriers to Success—Customer fulfillment continues to be a major stumbling block for e-tailers. Other barriers include: consumers reluctant to buy over the Internet due to security concerns, companies worried about cannibalization of brick and mortar store sales and increased price competition.

B. Direct marketing—Exposing a consumer to information about a good or service through a nonpersonal medium and convincing the customer to respond with an order.
   1. Mail order—Today, consumers can buy just about anything through the mail.
   2. Catalogues—Today, the catalogue customer is more likely to be an affluent career woman who has access to more than enough stores, but who does not have the time or desire to go to them.
   3. Direct Mail—A brochure or pamphlet offering a specific product or service at one point in time.

C. Direct Selling—Direct selling can be an effective approach, especially for products that require a great deal of information to sell.
   1. Door-to-Door Sales—Door-to-Door selling is declining markedly in the U.S. due to the large numbers of homes that are empty during the day due to the increase in working women, the increasing reluctance of those who are at home to admit strangers, and women feeling richer at the office.
   2. Parties and Networks—About three-quarters of direct sales are made in the consumer's home, sometimes at a home shopping party, at which a company representative makes a sales presentation to a group of people who have gathered in the home of a friend. In a multilevel network, a master distributor recruits other people to become distributors as well.
   3. Telemarketing—The use of telemarketing, where prospective customers are contacted by phone, is a cheaper and easier method.

D. Automatic Vending—Coin-operated vending machines are a tried-and-true way to sell convenience goods, especially cigarettes and drinks.

E. Direct-Response Television—As early as 1950, television brought retailing into the viewer's living room.
   1. Infomercials—Half-hour or hour commercials that resemble a talk show but are intended to sell something.
   2. Home Shopping Networks—Television channels that exist solely to sell products.

Key Terms

1.	Wheel of retailing hypothesis
2.	Retail life-cycle theory
3.	Traffic flow
4.	Inventory turnover
5.	Merchandise breadth
6.	Merchandise depth
7.	Supermarkets
8.	Specialty stores
9.	Department stores
10.	Hypermarkets
11.	Store image
12.	Nonstore retailing
13.	Direct marketing
14.	Multilevel network
15.	Point of Sale (POS) system

Multiple Choice

1.	c
2.	a
3.	b
4.	d
5.	d
6.	a
7.	c
8.	d
9.	b
10.	a
11.	a
12.	c
13.	d
14.	b
15.	c

Chapter in Review—Writing To Learn

1.   Retailers are classified by the merchandise assortment carried, that is, the assortment breadth and depth, are conveniences stores, supermarkets, specialty stores, discount stores, department stores, off price retailers, warehouse clubs and hypermarkets.

2.   Major types of retail locations include central business districts, secondary or neighbourhood business districts, shopping centres, freestanding retailers, and new nontraditional locations. Retailers, in making store location decisions consider many different factors including the number of competing stores in an area, the proximity to population centres, the cost of locating a store in an area, and, of course, their ability to make a profit at the new location.

3.   Critical success factors in e-tailing include strong branding, and the ability to build customer loyalty.

Case Analysis

1.   IKEA is based in Sweden but 70% of its sales come from beyond Scandinavia.

2.   IKEA's mission statement is: "IKEA shall offer a wide range of home furnishing items of good design and function, at prices so low, that the majority of people can afford to buy them."

4.   IKEA feared that if STR were to get a foothold in L.A., it could eventually expand and cause problems for IKEA in other trade areas.

5.   When selecting the site, IKEA considered the size of the location, and the image and reputation of the local community.

CHAPTER 16

Integrated Marketing Communications and Relationship Management

CHAPTER OVERVIEW

Marketers use a variety of communications tools to connect with customers. The four major elements of marketing communication are known as the communications mix, which includes personal selling, advertising, sales promotions, direct marketing and public relations. Marketers also communicate with customers through product and package design. Word-of-mouth communication from one consumer to another is often the most influential factor in consumer decisions.

Which communications mix elements will be used depends on the overall strategy, i.e., a push versus a pull strategy, the type of product, the stage of the product life cycle, and the degree of buyer readiness and the type of buyer. Communications budgets are often developed using rules of thumb; the specific strategies for the various mix elements are then planned and executed. Finally, marketers monitor and evaluate the communications efforts to determine if objectives are being reached.

The communications model describes the process by which a message source creates an idea, encodes the idea into a message, and transmits the message through some medium.

Relationship marketing is the philosophy and practice of developing long-term relationships with key stakeholders. Databases are used extensively to support relationship marketing efforts. Database marketing uses direct marketing tools and techniques to establish and develop ongoing customer relationships.

CHAPTER OBJECTIVES

1. Explain integrated marketing communications and its implementation, and why some marketers resist it.

2. List, describe and contrast the elements of the communications mix.

3. Explain the steps in developing a communications plan.

4.   Explain the philosophy and practices of relationship marketing.

5.   Explain the role of databases in facilitating marketing communications and relationship management.

CHAPTER OUTLINE

With reference to the textbook, please provide a brief description of each of the main elements listed in the Chapter Outline below. The page numbers will help guide you through the learning process.

I.   TAILORING MARKETING COMMUNICATIONS TO CUSTOMERS
        Promotion _____ *(p.444)*
        Marketing Communications _____ *(p.445)*

II.   COMMUNICATION STRATEGY
        A.   Integrated Communication Strategy _____ *(p.445)*
                1.   The Emerging IMC Perspective _____ *(p.446)*
                2.   Roadblocks to IMC _____ *(p.447)*
        B.   The Communications Mix
                1.   Advertising _____ *(p.448)*
                2.   Personal Selling_____ *(p.448)*
                3.   Direct Marketing_____ *(p.449)*
                4.   Public Relations _____ *(p.450)*
                5.   Sales Promotion _____ *(p.450)*
        C.   Developing a Communications Plan _____ *(p.451)*
                1.   Establish Communication Objectives
                        Create Awareness _____ *(p.452)*
                        Inform the Market_____ *(p.453)*
                        Create Desire_____ *(p.453)*
                        Encourage Trial_____ *(p.453)*
                        Build Loyalty _____ *(p.453)*
                2.   Identify Influences on the Communications Mix
                        Push Strategy_____ *(p.454)*
                        Pull Strategy _____ *(p.454)*
                        The Product Life Cycle _____ *(p.454)*
                3.   Determine and Allocate the Total Communication
                        Budget
                        Top-Down Budgeting Techniques _____ *(p.455)*
                        Percentage-of-Sales Method _____ *(p.455)*
                        Competitive-Parity Method_____ *(p.456)*
                        Bottom-Up Budgeting Techniques _____ *(p.456)*
                        Objective-Task Method_____ *(p.456)*

4.   Allocate the Budget to a Specific Communications Mix
      Organizational Factors _____ *(p.457)*
      Market Potential _____ *(p.457)*
      Market Size _____ *(p.457)*
5.   Evaluate the Effectiveness of the
      Communications Mix _____ *(p.457)*

III.   COMMUNICATION THEORY
       A.   The Communications Model _____ *(p.459)*
             1.   Encoding by the Marketer _____ *(p.459)*
             2.   The Source _____ *(p.459)*
             3.   The Message _____ *(p.460)*
                   AIDA Model _____ *(p.460)*
             4.   The Medium _____ *(p.460)*
             5.   Decoding by the Receiver
                   Receiver _____ *(p.461)*
                   Decoding _____ *(p.461)*
             6.   Noise _____ *(p.461)*
             7.   Feedback _____ *(p.461)*
       B.   Relationship Marketing
             1.   CRM _____ *(p.462)*
             2.   Database Marketing _____ *(p.463)*
             3.   Other Relationship Marketing Tools _____ *(p.465)*

KEY TERMS

Select the correct term for each definition and write it in the space provided.

Communications mix   Push strategy
Integrated marketing communications (IMC)   Message
Decoding   Promotion
Communications plan   Communications model
Source   Interactive marketing
Database marketing   Medium
Pull strategy   Customer relationship marketing (CRM)
Noise

1. _____   The coordination of a marketer's communications efforts to influence attitudes or behaviour toward a product or services *(p. 444)*

2. _____   The use of direct marketing tools and techniques to establish and develop ongoing customer relationships. *(p.464)*

3. _____   A strategic business process that marketers use to plan, develop, execute and evaluate coordinated, measurable, persuasive communications over time with targeted audiences. *(p.460)*

4. _____   The major elements of marketer-controlled communications including advertising, sales promotions, direct marketing, public relations, and personal selling. *(p.447)*

5. _____   Relationship marketing focused on delivering customer satisfaction and improved customer retention. *(p.462)*

6. _____   The elements necessary for meaning to be transferred from a sender to a receiver. *(p. 459)*

7. _____   A framework that outlines the strategies for developing, implementing and controlling the firm's communications activities. *(p.451)*

8. _____   Moving products through the channel by convincing channel members to offer them. *(p. 454)*

9. _____   Moving products through the channel by building desire for the products among consumers who convince retailers to stock the items. *(p.454)*

10. _____   An organization or individual that sends a message. *(p.459)*

11. _____   The communication in physical form that goes from a sender to a receiver. *(p.460)*

12. _____ A communications vehicle through which a
message is transmitted to a target audience.
(p.461)

13. _____ The process by which a receiver assigns
meaning to the message. *(p.461)*

14. _____ Anything that interferes with effective
communication. *(p.461)*

15. _____ Two-way communications in which
customized marketing communications elicit
a measurable response from individual
receivers. *(p.449)*

MULTIPLE CHOICE

Identify the most correct answer.

1. Promotion: *(p.444)*
   a. informs consumers about new goods and services, and where they can be obtained.
   b. reminds consumers to continue using familiar products.
   c. builds relationships with customers.
   d. all of the above.

2. Nonpersonal communication that is paid for by an identified sponsor using mass media to inform or persuade an audience is: *(p.448)*
   a. sales promotion.
   b. publicity.
   c. advertising.
   d. campaigning.

3. Public relations activities include: *(p.450)*
   a. press releases.
   b. staged events.
   c. responding to product recalls.
   d. all of the above.

4. When a company focuses on getting journalists to develop stories about their products, they are seeking: *(p.450)*
   a. an anonymous expert to advertise the product.
   b. public relations.
   c. publicity.
   d. none of the above.

5. When interest is heightened by not revealing the exact nature of the product, this is known as a(n): *(p.452)*
    a.   teaser campaign.
    b.   infomercial.
    c.   private promotion.
    d.   ghost advertisement.

6. Communications efforts must start to focus on communicating specific product benefits in the: *(p.454)*
    a.   introduction phase.
    b.   growth phase.
    c.   maturity phase.
    d.   decline phase.

7. The most commonly used top-down budgeting procedure, in which the communications budget is based on either last year's sales or on estimates of this year's sales, is called: *(p.455)*
    a.   all-you-can-afford method.
    b.   competitive-parity method.
    c.   objective-task method.
    d.   percentage-of-sales method.

8. Using this bottom-up budgeting approach, the firm first defines the specific communication goals it hopes to achieve, then tries to figure to how much and what kind of communications efforts it would take to meet that goal. *(p.456)*
    a.   All-you-can-afford method.
    b.   Competitive-parity method.
    c.   Objective-task method.
    d.   Percentage-of-sales method.

9. The process of translating an idea into a form of communication that will convey meaning is called: *(p.459)*
    a.   descriptive analysis.
    b.   decoding.
    c.   semiotics.
    d.   encoding.

10. An advertising strategy where a message contains both positive and negative information is called: *(p.460)*
    a.   conclusive advertising.
    b.   a two-sided message.
    c.   representative advertising.
    d.   a one-sided message.

11.   The organization or individual that intercepts and interprets the message is known as the: *(p.461)*

     a.   messenger.

     b.   decoder.

     c.   receiver.

     d.   medium.

12.   The reactions of the receiver to the message, which are communicated back to the source, are referred to as: *(p.461)*

     a.   feedback.

     b.   interactions.

     c.   appeals.

     d.   effectiveness.

13.   The philosophy and practice of developing long-term relationships with key stakeholders is called: *(p.462)*

     a.   interactive marketing.

     b.   relationship marketing.

     c.   customer relationship marketing.

     d.   the AIDA model.

14.   Other relationship marketing tools include: *(p.465)*

     a.   loyalty programs.

     b.   advertising.

     c.   promotion.

     d.   all of the above.

15.   Database marketing helps marketers achieve which of the following objectives: *(p.464)*

     a.   locate new customers.

     b.   stimulate cross selling.

     c.   provide measurable results.

     d.   all of the above.

CHAPTER IN REVIEW—WRITING TO LEARN

1.   Explain the goals of marketing communications.

_____

_____

_____

_____

2.   List and describe the elements of the communications mix.

_____

_____

_____

_____

3.   Describe database marketing and how marketers use it to satisfy customers.

_____

_____

_____

_____

CASE ANALYSIS

Real People, Real Decisions: David Edward, Cormark Communications

Reread the three sections comprising the Cormark Communications vignette in Chapter 16 and answer the following questions:

1.   As a full service agency, what types of services does Cormark offer its clients?

2.   Which industries does Cormark target?

3.   What are Cormark and Pfizer's communications objectives with respect to the launch of Rimadyl in Canada?

4.   What is the advantage of investing in a "made in Canada" solution for Rimadyl?

SCENARIO

You are the Assistant Vice President of Marketing of a large credit union in Western Canada. You have become increasingly convinced that your institution should invest in improving its customer database. Currently, your database does not provide a full picture of all products held by each client. Your mortgage system contains only mortgage information, and so forth. Considerable investment is required to integrate these disparate databases. To convince your boss that the investment is worth it, you begin to ponder the following questions:

1. How will an integrated customer database help you to communicate more effectively with your existing customers?
2. How will an integrated customer database stimulate cross-selling?
3. How can an integrated customer database allow you to create more effective marketing campaigns—and how will you *know* they are more effective?
4. How can an integrated customer database help you identify new customers?

ANSWERS

Chapter Outline

I. TAILORING MARKETING COMMUNICATIONS TO CUSTOMERS
    Promotion—The coordination of a marketer's marketing communications efforts to influence attitudes or behaviour toward a product or service.
    Marketing Communications—Informing consumers and customers about the relative value of products, and developing trust and other relational bonds that facilitate ongoing exchange relationships.

II. COMMUNICATION STRATEGY
    A. The Communications Mix—The major elements of marketer-controlled communications including advertising, sales promotions, marketing public relations, direct marketing and personal selling.
        1. Advertising—Nonpersonal communication from an identified sponsor, primarily using mass media.
        2. Personal Selling—Direct interaction between a company representative and a customer, which can occur in person, by phone, or even over an interactive computer link.
        3. Direct Marketing—Catalogues, direct mail, the Internet and direct response TV are tools of direct marketing.
        4. Public Relations—Seeking a positive image for the product or company through press releases, staging events, and commissioning surveys.
        5. Sales Promotion—Contests or store demonstrations designed to build interest in a specified product in a specified time.

    B. Managing The Communications Mix
        Communications Plan—A framework that outlines the strategies for developing, implementing, and controlling the firm's communications activities.
        1. Establish Communications Objectives
            Create Awareness—Make members of the target market aware that a new brand is available in the market.
            Inform the Market—Provide prospective users with knowledge about the benefits the new product has to offer.
            Create Desire—Create favourable feelings toward the product, and convince some to use the product.
            Encourage Trial—The company now needs to get consumers who have expressed interest in the product to try it.
            Build Loyalty—Convince customers to keep buying the product.
        2. Identify Influences on Communications Mix
            Push Strategy—The company tries to move its products through the channel by convincing channel members to offer them.
            Pull Strategy—The company tries to move its products through the channel by building desire for the products among consumers, thus convincing retailers to respond to this demand by stocking those items.
            The Product Life Cycle Influences Communications Mix—Introduction Phase-build awareness. Growth phase—focus on specific benefits of product. Maturity Phase-many people have tried product, sales promotion should increase. Decline phase—as sales fall, spending on communications is reduced.

3.   Determine and Allocate the Total Communications Budget
Top-Down Budgeting Techniques—Allocation of the communications budget based on the total amount to be devoted to marketing communications.
Percentage-of-Sales Method—A method for communications budgeting in which the communications budget is based on a certain percentage of either last year's sales or on estimates for the present year's sales.
Competitive-Parity Method—Spending what competitors spend on communications.
Bottom-Up Budgeting Techniques—Allocation of the communications budget based on identifying communications goals and allocating enough money to accomplish them.
Objective-Task Method—A budgeting method in which an organization first defines the specific communication goals it hopes to achieve and then tries to calculate what kind of communications efforts it will take to meet these goals.

4.   Allocate the Budget to a Specific Mix
Organizational Factors—Preferences within the company based on past experiences or specific goals.
Market Potential—Allocate more resources in markets where consumers will be more likely to buy the product.
Market Size—Larger markets are more expensive places in which to promote.

5.   Evaluate the Effectiveness of the Communications Mix
Monitor and evaluate the company's communications efforts.

III.   COMMUNICATION THEORY

A.   The Communications Model
Communications Model—The elements necessary for meaning to be transferred from a sender to a receiver.

1.   Encoding by the Marketer—The process of translating an idea into a form of communication that will convey meaning.

2.   The Source—An organization or individual that sends a message.

3.   The Message—The communication in physical form which is sent from a sender to a receiver.
AIDA Model—The communications goals of attention, interest, desire, and action.

4.   The Medium—A communications vehicle through which a message is transmitted to target audience.

5.   Decoding by the Receiver
Receiver—The organization or individual that intercepts and interprets the message.
Decoding—The process of assigning meaning to the message by a receiver.

6.   Noise—Anything that interferes with effective communication.

7.   Feedback—The reactions of the receiver to the message that are communicated back to the source.

B.   Relationship Marketing—The philosophy and practice of developing long-term relationships with key stakeholders.

1.   CRM—Relationship marketing focused on delivering customer satisfaction and improved customer retention.

2.   Database Marketing—The creation of an ongoing relationship with a set of customers who have an identifiable interest in a product or service, and whose responses to communications efforts become part of future communications attempts.

3.   Other relationship marketing tools—Includes a wide range of vehicles, such as e-mail, newsletters, and recognition or loyalty programs.

Key Terms

1. Promotion
2. Database marketing
3. Integrated marketing communications (IMC)
4. Communications mix
5. Transactional data
6. Communications model
7. Communications plan
8. Push strategy
9. Pull strategy
10. Source
11. Message
12. Medium
13. Decoding
14. Noise
15. Interactive marketing

Multiple Choice

1. d
2. c
3. d
4. c
5. a
6. b
7. d
8. c
9. d
10. b
11. c
12. a
13. b
14. a
15. d

Chapter in Review—Writing To Learn

1. Marketers use a variety of communications tools to connect with customers. Through communications strategies marketers inform consumers about new products, remind them of familiar products, persuade them to choose one alternative over another, and build strong relationships with customers.

2. Personal selling provides face-to-face contact between a company representative and customer. Advertising is nonpersonal communication from an identified sponsor using mass media. Sales promotions stimulate immediate sales by providing incentives to the trade or to consumers. Publicity and public relations activities seek to influence the attitude of various publics.

3. Database marketing is interactive marketing that utilizes a customized database. Database marketing allows marketers to develop dialogues and build relationships with customers. Marketers use database marketing to create programs that are more flexible, reward loyal users, locate new customers, offer related products to existing customers, i.e., cross-selling, and track customer responses.

Case Analysis

1. As a full-service agency, Cormark offers its clients: communications counsel, strategic planning, advertising, promotion and direct marketing planning and execution.

2. Cormark currently targets the following industries: financial services, life sciences, agricultural, business-to-business, packaged goods and retail.

3. At the product launch stage, creating awareness is the main communication objective.

4. The advantage of a "made in Canada" solution is that the project would be managed to Canadian standards and Canadian expectations.

CHAPTER 17

Advertising

CHAPTER OVERVIEW

The main purpose of this chapter is to explain advertising's role in marketing communications. Advertising is nonpersonal communication from an identified sponsor using mass media to persuade or influence an audience. The major types of advertising are consumer product advertising, trade advertising, and institutional advertising. Advertising begins with the client or advertiser who may be a manufacturer, a distributor, a retailer, or an institution. Advertising agencies create ads or other promotions and arrange for their delivery to the target market.

Planning of an advertising campaign begins with developing objectives. Next, advertisers develop a creative strategy that should create attention, interest, desire, and action. A media plan determines where and when advertising will appear. Broadcast media include television and radio. Print media refers to newspapers, magazines, and directories. In developing media schedules, planners consider the size and characteristics of each media vehicle's audience, the objectives of the media plan, the advertising of competitors, and the capabilities of the media.

While we can be confident that, in general, advertising does increase sales, advertisers need to conduct research to determine if specific advertisements are effective. Examples of types of research include pretesting or copy testing of advertising before placing it in the media and posttesting research.

Finally, there are important considerations in advertising to international markets. A standardized strategy may be used where the same ad campaign is used in different cultures and emphasizes similarities of consumers.

CHAPTER OBJECTIVES

1.   Tell what advertising is and describe the major types of advertising.

2.   Describe the major players in the advertising process.

3.   Tell how advertisers develop an advertising campaign.

4.   Describe the major advertising media and the important considerations in media planning.

5. Explain how advertisers evaluate the effectiveness of the campaign.

6. Discuss the challenges facing advertising.

CHAPTER OUTLINE

With reference to the textbook, please provide a brief description of each of the main elements listed in the Chapter Outline below. The page numbers will help guide you through the learning process.

I. PROMOTIONAL MESSAGES: AND NOW A WORD
    FROM OUR SPONSOR…
    Advertising_____ *(p.474)*
    A. Types of Advertising
        1. Product Advertising _____ *(p.474)*
        2. Institutional Advertising _____ *(p.475)*
            Advocacy Advertising_____ *(p.475)*
            Public Service Advertisements _____ *(p.475)*
    B. Who Does Advertising? _____ *(p.475)*
        Advertising Campaign_____ *(p.475)*
        In-House Agency_____ *(p.475)*
        Limited Service Agency _____ *(p.475)*
        Full-Service Agency _____ *(p.475)*
        1. Account Management _____ *(p.476)*
        2. Creative Services_____ *(p.477)*
        3. Research and Marketing Services _____ *(p.477)*
        4. Media Planning_____ *(p.477)*

II. DEVELOPING THE ADVERTISING CAMPAIGN
    A. Identify The Target Market _____ *(p.478)*
    B. Establish Message and Budget Objectives _____ *(p.478)*
        1. Setting Message Goals _____ *(p.477)*
        2. Setting the Budget_____ *(p.479)*
    C. Design The Ad
        Creative Strategy _____ *(p.479)*
        Advertising Appeal _____ *(p.479)*
        1. Common Advertising Appeals
            Reasons Why: The Unique Selling Proposition _____ *(p.480)*
            Comparative Advertising _____ *(p.480)*
            Demonstration_____ *(p.480)*
            Testimonial _____ *(p.480)*
            Slice-of-Life _____ *(p.480)*
            Lifestyle_____ *(p.481)*

                Fear Appeals _____ *(p.481)*
                Sex Appeals_____ *(p.481)*
                Humourous Appeals _____ *(p.481)*
    D.   Pretest What Will Be Said
                Pretesting _____ *(p.481)*
                Copy Testing _____ *(p.481)*
                Copy Testing Techniques _____ *(p.481)*
    E.   Choose The Media
                Media Planning _____ *(p.482)*
                Aperture_____ *(p.482)*
            1.   Types of Media: Where to Say It _____ *(p.483)*
                        Television _____ *(p.484)*
                          Radio _____ *(p.484)*
                        Newspapers_____ *(p.484)*
                        Magazines _____ *(p.484)*
                        Directories_____ *(p.484)*
                        Computer Media _____ *(p.484)*
                        Out-of-Home Media _____ *(p.485)*
             2.   Media Scheduling: When to Say It
                        Media Schedule_____ *(p.485)*
                        Advertising Exposure _____ *(p.486)*
                        Impressions _____ *(p.486)*
                        Reach_____ *(p.486)*
                        Frequency _____ *(p.486)*
                        Gross Rating Points_____ *(p.486)*
                        Cost Per Thousand _____ *(p.487)*
             3.   Media Scheduling: How Often to Say It _____ *(p.487)*

III.   EVALUATING ADVERTISING
    A.   Pretesting_____ *(p.488)*
                Unaided Recall _____ *(p.489)*
                 Aided Recall _____ *(p.489)*
                Attitudinal Measures _____ *(p.489)*
    B.   Challenges Facing the Advertising Industry _____ *(p.489)*
    C.   How the Advertising Industry is Meeting the Challenges_____ *(p.490)*

KEY TERMS

Select the correct term for each definition and write it in the space provided.

Reach
Unique Selling Proposition (USP)
Advertising
Cost per thousand (CPM)
Creative strategy
Advertising appeal
Media schedule
Advocacy advertising

Media planning
Copy testing
Aided recall
Gross Rating Points (GRPs)
Product advertising
Frequency
Advertising campaign

1. _____ Nonpersonal communication paid for by an identified sponsor using mass media to persuade or inform. *(p.474)*

2. _____ An advertising message that focuses on a specific good or service. *(p.474)*

3. _____ A type of public-service advertising provided by an organization seeking to influence public opinion on an issue in which it has some stake in the outcome. *(p.475)*

4. _____ A coordinated, comprehensive communications plan that carries out promotion objectives and results in a series of advertisements placed in media over a period of time. *(p.475)*

5. _____ A research technique that uses clue to prompt answers from people about advertisements they might have seen. *(p.489)*

6. _____ The central idea or theme of an advertising message. *(p.479)*

7. _____ An advertising appeal that focuses on one clear reason why a particular product is superior to any others. *(p.480)*

8. _____ The process that turns a concept into an advertisement. *(p.479)*

9. _____ The process of developing media objectives, strategies, and tactics for use in an advertising campaign. *(p.482)*

10. _____ The plan that specifies the exact media to use and when. *(p.485)*

11. _____ The percentage of the target market that will be exposed to the media vehicle. *(p.486)*

12. _____ The number of times a person in the target group will be exposed to the message. *(p.486)*

13. _____ A measure used for comparing the effectiveness of different media vehicles; average reach times frequency. *(p.487)*

14. _____ A measure used to compare the relative cost-effectiveness of different media vehicles that have different exposure rates; the cost to deliver a message to 1000 people or homes. *(p.487)*

15. _____ A marketing research method that seeks to measure the effectiveness of ads by determining whether consumers are receiving, comprehending and responding to the ad according to plan. *(p.481)*

MULTIPLE CHOICE

Identify the most correct answer.

1. In ancient Greece and Rome, advertisements of sorts appeared on: *(p.474)*
   a. walls and tablets.
   b. vases.
   c. tree trunks.
   d. togas.

2. Product advertising usually has the following purpose(s): *(p.474)*
   a. Educates people about a new product and what it does.
   b. Emphasizes a brand's features and tries to convince the target market to choose it over other options.
   c. Ensures that people won't forget about the product.
   d. All of the above.

3. On average, Canadian businesses spend this much on advertising annually: *(p.474)*
   a. 600 million.
   b. 1 billion.
   c. 6 billion.
   d. 60 billion.

4. Advertising that promotes the activities, personality or point of view of an organization or company is called: *(p.475)*
   a. business-to-business advertising.
   b. product advertising.
   c. institutional advertising.
   d. retail advertising.

5. Advocacy advertising is designed to: *(p.475)*
   a. create or enhance brand image.
   b. increase the distribution of products by persuading more retailers to carry them.
   c. influence public opinion on an issue of public service.
   d. none of the above.

6. Rather than focusing on a specific good or service, institutional advertising promotes: *(p.474)*
   a. the activities, "personality", or point of view of an organization.
   b. communication between manufacturers and businesses and organizations.
   c. an issue that is clearly in the public interest.
   d. the store's location, hours, price, and the availability of certain products.

7. An advertising campaign: *(p.475)*
   a. shares the cost of local advertising with a retailer.
   b. results in a series of advertisements placed in media over a period of time.
   c. evaluates the standing of different media vehicles in terms of their ability to deliver it to the desired consumer group.
   d. all of the above.

8. A disadvantage of television advertising is: *(p.483)*
   a. the reproduction quality of images is relatively poor.
   b. it reaches a large audience.
   c. hard to communicate complex messages.
   d. the audience is increasingly fragmented.

9. The account executive of an advertising agency: *(p.476)*
   a. is the person who actually dreams up and produces the ads.
   b. assists in designing and evaluating ad executions.
   c. is in charge of developing the campaign strategy for the client and ensuring that the advertising that is created will meet the client's desired objectives.
   d. all of the above.

10. To compare the relative cost-effectiveness of different media and of spots run on different vehicles in the same medium, media planners use a measure called: *(p.487)*
    a. cost per thousand (CPM).
    b. reach.
    c. effective demand.
    d. gross rating points (GRPs).

11. An aperture is: *(p.482)*
    a. the process that occurs when a concept is translated into an actual advertisement.
    b. the best place and time to reach a person in the target market group.
    c. the central idea of the message.
    d. the information to be presented about an item.

12. Comparative advertising is when: *(p.480)*
    a. the negative consequences of using or not using a product are highlighted.
    b. celebrity endorsers are used to differentiate a product from competitors.
    c. an emotional response in the receiver creates a desire for the product.
    d. two or more brands are compared by name.

13. The testimonial format of presenting information in an advertisement involves: *(p.480)*
    a. a speech where the source speaks directly to the audience in an attempt to inform them about a product or idea.
    b. the use of comparison, where the reader is told "A is B".
    c. a story about an abstract trait or concept that has been personified as a person, animal, vegetable, or mythical character.
    d. a celebrity, an expert, or a "typical person" stating how effective the product is.

14. Demonstration advertisements: *(p.480)*
    a. are commercial messages arranged according to interest or topic.
    b. are inserts in the newspaper.
    c. consist of a product "in action" to prove it performs.
    d. explicitly name two or more competitors.

15. To calculate the exposure a message will have if placed in a certain medium, planners measure exposure by considering two factors: *(p.486)*
    a. reach and frequency.
    b. sales pattern and attention.
    c. quality and quantity.
    d. size and conveyance.

CHAPTER IN REVIEW—WRITING TO LEARN

1.   Explain advertising's role in marketing goals.

        _____

        _____

        _____

        _____

2.   List and describe the major types of advertising.

        _____

        _____

        _____

        _____

3.   Explain some of the important considerations in media planning.

        _____

        _____

        _____

        _____

CASE ANALYSIS

Real People, Real Decision: Anna Olofsson, A&O Analys

Reread the three sections comprising the A&O Analys vignette in Chapter 17 and answer the following questions:

1.   What type of advertisements did the Swedish Brewers Association ask Olofsson to create?

2.   What type of appeals were considered for the new ads?

3.   Which media vehicle did the Swedish Brewers Association elect to use?

4.   What did the posttesting after the campaign reveal?

SCENARIO

You are Director of the "Creatives" in a large Canadian advertising agency. You and an agency account executive have just met with a new client, a small Canadian microbrewery that produces a line of specialty beers targeted to the upscale baby boomer market. Until now, the company's beer has only been promoted and distributed through clubs and bars, but the client is now ready to launch nationally in liquor and/or beer distribution outlets across Canada. Your client has asked you to develop ideas for the microbrewery's first ever advertising campaign. You and the staff are asked to come back with four distinct campaigns, using any combination of newspaper, magazine, billboard, radio or television as media. However, the client has specified that you must explore the use of four different appeals. Develop one campaign for each of the following appeals, and make a media recommendation that complements the appeal selected.

1.   "Reasons why" appeal.
2.   Comparative advertising appeal.
3.   Testimonial.
4.   Lifestyle.

ANSWERS

Chapter Outline

I.   PROMOTIONAL MESSAGES: AND NOW A WORD FROM OUR SPONSOR...
Advertising—Nonpersonal communication paid for by an identified sponsor using mass media to persuade or inform.
     A.   Types of Advertising
          1.   Product Advertising—An advertising message that focuses on a specific good or service.
          2.   Institutional Advertising—An advertising message that promotes the activities, personality, or point of view of an organization or company.
                 Advocacy Advertising—A type of public service advertising provided by an organization that is seeking to influence public opinion on an issue because it has some stake in the outcome.
                 Public Service Advertising—Advertising run by the media without charge for not-for-profit organizations or to champion a particular cause.
     B.   Who Does Advertising?—Creating and executing an advertising campaign often means many companies work together, and it requires a broad range of skilled people to do the job right.
            Advertising Campaign—A coordinated, comprehensive plan that carries out promotion objectives and results in a series of advertisements placed in media over a period of time.
            In-House Agency—Firms that do their own advertising.
            Limited-Service Agency—Provides one or more specialized services such as media buying or creative development.
            Full-Service Agency—Provides most or all of the services needed to mount a campaign, including research, creation of ad copy and art, media selection, and production of the final messages.
          1.   Account Management—The account executive or account manager develops the campaign's strategy for the client.
          2.   Creative Services—Creatives are the "heart" of the communications effort. They dream up and produce the ads.
          3.   Research and Marketing Services—Researchers are the "brains" of the campaign. They collect and analyze the data.
          4.   Media Planning—Determines which communication vehicles are the most effective and efficient.

II.   DEVELOPING THE ADVERTISING CAMPAIGN
     A.   Identify the Target Market—The target market is identified from research and segmentation decisions.
     B.   Establish Message and Budget Objectives—Advertising objectives should be consistent with the marketing plan.
          1.   Setting Message Goals—Message goals can be increasing brand awareness, boosting sales by a certain percentage or even changing the image of a product.
          2.   Setting the Budget—The major approaches and techniques include the percentage-of-sales and objective-task methods.
     C.   Design The Ad
            Creative Strategy—The process that turns a concept into an advertisement.
            Advertising Appeal—The central idea or theme of an advertising message.
          1.   Common Advertising Appeals
                 Reasons Why: The Unique Selling Proposition—An advertising appeal that focuses on one clear reason why a particular product is superior.
                 Comparative Advertising—Explicitly names two or more competitors.
                 Demonstration—The ad shows a product "in action" to prove that it performs as claimed.
                 Testimonial—A celebrity, an expert, or a "typical person" states the product's effectiveness.
                 Slice-of-Life—The format presents a (dramatized) scene from everyday life.

Lifestyle—This format shows a person or persons attractive to the target market in an appealing setting.

Fear Appeals—The negative consequences of using or not using a product.

Sex Appeals—Some ads appear to be selling sex rather than products.

Humourous Appeals—Can be an effective way to break through advertising clutter.

D.   Pretest What Will Be Said

Pretesting—A research method that seeks to minimize mistakes by getting consumer reactions to ad messages before they are placed in the media.

Copy Testing—A marketing research method that seeks to measure ad effectiveness by determining whether consumers are receiving, comprehending, and responding to the ad according to plan.

Copy Testing Techniques—Concept Testing, Test Commercials, and Finished Testing.

E.   Choose the Media

Media Planning—The process of developing media objectives, strategies, and tactics for use in an advertising campaign.

Aperture—The best place and time to reach a person in the target market group.

1.   Types of Media: Where to Say It—The major categories of media.

Television—The ability to reach many people at once.

Radio—Flexible, low cost, and the ability to reach specific consumer segments.

Newspapers—An excellent medium for local advertising.

Magazines—Flexibility and wide readership.

Directories—The most "down-to-earth" information focused advertising.

Computer Media—A communication medium that transmits information through the Internet or via e-mail messages.

Out-of-Home Media—A communication medium that reaches people in public places.

2.   Media Scheduling: When to Say It

Media Schedule—The plan that specifies the exact media to be used and when.

Advertising Exposure—The degree to which the target market will see an advertising message placed in a specific vehicle.

Impressions—The number of people who will be exposed to a message placed in one or more media vehicles.

Reach—The percentage of the target market that will be exposed to the media vehicle.

Frequency—The number of times a person in the target group will be exposed to the message.

Gross Rating Points—Measure used for comparing the effectiveness of different media vehicles; average reach times frequency.

Cost Per Thousand—Measure that compares the relative cost effectiveness of different media vehicles with different exposure rates; cost to deliver a message to 1000 people or homes.

3.   Media Scheduling: How Often To Say It—A continuous schedule, or pulsing schedule.

III.   EVALUATING ADVERTISING

A.   Posttesting—Research conducted on consumers' responses to actual advertising messages they have seen or heard.

Unaided Recall—A research technique conducted by telephone survey or personal interview that asks how much of an ad a person remembers during a specified period of time.

Aided Recall—A research technique that uses clues to prompt answers from people about advertisements they might have seen.

Attitudinal Measures—A research technique that probes a consumer's beliefs or feelings about a product before and after being exposed to messages about it.

B.   Challenges Facing The Advertising Industry—An erosion of brand loyalty. Technology gives power back to the people. Greater emphasis on point-of-purchase factors. The rules are changing. The advertising environment is cluttered. Some consumers are turned off by advertising.

C.   How the Advertising Industry is Meeting the Challenges—Establish a global reach, reflect diversity, and embrace technology.

Key Terms

1. Advertising
2. Product advertising
3. Advocacy advertising
4. Advertising campaign
5. Aided recall
6. Advertising appeal
7. Unique Selling Proposition (USP)
8. Creative strategy
9. Media planning
10. Media schedule
11. Reach
12. Frequency
13. Gross Rating Points (GRPs)
14. Cost per thousand (CPM)
15. Copy testing

Multiple Choice

1. a
2. d
3. c
4. c
5. c
6. a
7. b
8. d
9. c
10. a
11. b
12. d
13. d
14. c
15. a

Chapter in Review—Writing To Learn

1. Advertising is nonpersonal communication from an identified sponsor using mass media to persuade or influence an audience. Advertising informs, reminds, and creates consumer desire. Advertising allows the organization to communicate its message in a favourable way and to repeat the message as often as it deems necessary for it to have impact on receivers.

2. Product advertising is used to persuade consumers to choose a specific product or brand. Institutional advertising is used to promote an entire organization (corporate image advertising), express the opinions of an organization (advocacy advertising), or to support a case (public service advertising).

3. In developing media schedules, planners consider the size and characteristics of each media vehicle's audience, the objectives of the media plan (i.e., reach and frequency), the advertising of competitors, and the capabilities of the media. In comparing different media, planners examine the comparative cost efficiency of each media vehicle i.e., cost per thousand (CPM). Media planners must also decide when to deliver the messages or whether to use a continuous, pulsing, or flighting schedule.

Case Analysis

1. Olofsson produced public service announcements.

2. The appeal to fear was the main one considered, although the campaign did eventually incorporating both fear and humour appeals.

3. Television was the main medium selected, but it was complemented with personal appearances and a magazine.

4. Posttesting revealed that 89% of those who received the magazine read at least parts of it. Ninety two percent thought the campaign was trustworthy, 76% said it made them think about how their friends used alcohol, and half said it made them think about their own drinking habits.

CHAPTER 18

Sales Promotion, Public Relations, and Personal Selling

CHAPTER OVERVIEW

In this chapter, we first reviewed the purpose of public relations to maintain or improve the image of an organization among various publics. An important part of this is managing publicity. Public relations is important in introducing new products, influencing legislation, enhancing the image of a city, region or country, and calling attention to a firm's community involvement.

Next, we described the steps in developing a public relations campaign which begin with setting promotional objectives, examining the current attitudes of various publics, determining the issues of interest, and then planning what action to take. A PR campaign may include sponsorship of an event, cause-related marketing activities, and developing print or video news releases about timely topics.

Sales promotions are short-term programs designed to build interest in or encourage purchase of a product. Trade promotions include merchandise allowances, push money, trade shows, promotional products, and incentive programs.

Personal selling occurs when a company representative directly informs a client about a good or service to get a sale. Personal selling is more important for push strategies. Because of the high cost per customer contact, telemarketing is growing in popularity. Different types of salespeople include order takers, technical specialists, missionary salespeople, and order getters.

The steps in the personal selling process include prospecting, qualifying the prospects, the preapproach, the approach, making the sales presentation, overcoming customer objections, closing the sale, and follow up after the sale.

Finally, sales management means planning, implementing, and controlling the selling function. The responsibilities of a sales manager are setting sales force objectives and creating a sales force strategy, including specifying sales territories, recruiting, training, and rewarding salespeople.

CHAPTER OBJECTIVES

1.   Explain the role of public relations.

2.   Describe the steps in developing a public relations campaign.

3.   Explain what sales promotion is and describe some of the different types of trade and consumer sales promotion activities.

4.   Explain the important role of personal selling in the marketing effort.

5.   List the steps in the personal selling process.

6.   Explain the job of the sales manager.

CHAPTER OUTLINE

With reference to the textbook, please provide a brief description of each of the main elements listed in the Chapter Outline below. The page numbers will help guide you through the learning process.

I.   ADVERTISING'S NOT THE ONLY GAME IN TOWN! _____ *(p.498)*

II.   PUBLIC RELATIONS _____ *(p.499)*
A.   Objectives of Public Relations
        1.   Introducing New Products_____ *(p.500)*
        2.   Supporting Current Products_____ *(p.500)*
        3.   Influencing Government Legislation _____ *(p.500)*
        4.   Enhancing the Image of an Organization or Entity___ *(p.500)*
        5.   Calling Attention to a Firm's Involvement
                in the Community _____ *(p.500)*
        6.   Demonstrating Social Responsibility _____ *(p.500)*
        7.   Developing Positive Employee or Investor Relations *(p.500)*
        8.   Handling Communications Issues and Crises _____ *(p.500)*
B.   Planning a Public Relations Campaign
        1.   Tools _____ *(p.502)*
        2.   Publicity _____ *(p.502)*
        3.   Press Release_____ *(p.502)*

III. SALES PROMOTION _____ *(p.506)*
    A.   Trade Promotion
        1.   Discounts and Deals _____ *(p.506)*
            Merchandise Allowance _____ *(p.506)*
            Case Allowance_____ *(p.506)*
        2.   Industry Boosting and Boasting
            Trade Shows _____ *(p.506)*
            Promotional Products _____ *(p.507)*
            Incentive Programs _____ *(p.508)*
            Push Money_____ *(p.508)*
    B.   Consumer Promotions
        1.   Price-Based Consumer Promotions_____ *(p.508)*
            Coupons _____ *(p.508)*
            Rebates _____ *(p.508)*
            Special Packs_____ *(p.508)*
        2.   Attention-Getting Consumer Promotions _____ *(p.508)*
            Contests and Sweepstakes_____ *(p.508)*
            Premiums _____ *(p.509)*
            Sampling_____ *(p.509)*
            Point-of-Purchase (POP) Promotion_____ *(p.509)*
            Continuity, Membership & Loyalty Programs _____ *(p.509)*
            Cross-Promotion_____ *(p.509)*

IV. PERSONAL SELLING_____ *(p.511)*
    A.   The Role of Personal Selling
        Telemarketing _____ *(p.511)*
        Order Taker _____ *(p.511)*
        Technical Specialist_____ *(p.512)*
        Missionary Salesperson_____ *(p.512)*
        Order Getter_____ *(p.512)*
    B.   Approaches to Personal Selling_____ *(p.512)*
        1.   Transactional Marketing: Putting on the Hard Sell
            Transactional Selling_____ *(p.512)*
        2.   Relationship Selling: Countering the Tarnished Image
            Relationship Selling _____ *(p.512)*
    C.   The Role of Personal Selling in the Communications Mix___ *(p.513)*

D. The Selling Process _____ *(p.513)*
   Creative Selling Process _____ *(p.513)*
   1. Prospect Customers
      Prospecting _____ *(p.513)*
   2. Qualify Prospects _____ *(p.513)*
   3. Do a Preapproach _____ *(p.514)*
   4. Make the Approach_____ *(p.514)*
   5. Make the Sales Presentation _____ *(p.514)*
   6. Overcome Customer Objections _____ *(p.515)*
   7. Close the Sale _____ *(p.515)*
   8. Follow-Up After the Sale _____ *(p.515)*
E. Sales Management_____ *(p.515)*
   1. Setting Sales Force Objectives _____ *(p.515)*
   2. Creating a Sales Force Strategy _____ *(p.516)*
      Sales Territory_____ *(p.516)*
   3. Recruiting, Training, and Rewarding Salespeople
      Recruiting _____ *(p.516)*
      Sales Training _____ *(p.516)*
      Rewarding Salespeople _____ *(p.516)*

KEY TERMS

Select the correct term for each definition and write it in the space provided.

Rebate

Premium

Publicity

Sales promotion

Telemarketing

Order getter

Order taker

Point-of-purchase (POP)

Coupons

Price deal

Qualify prospects

Public relations

Case allowance

Merchandise allowance

Press release

1. _____   A program designed to build interest in or encourage purchase of a product or service during a specified time period. *(p.506)*

2. _____   A type of sales trade promotion that reimburses the retailer for in-store support or the product. *(p.506)*

3. _____   A part of the selling process that determines how likely prospects are to become customers. *(p.514)*

4. _____ An items included without charge with a purchased product. *(p.509)*

5. _____ The use of displays or signs to influence purchases at the store. *(p.509)*

6. _____ Certificates redeemable for money off on a purchase. *(p.508)*

7. _____ A salesperson who works creatively to develop relationships with customers or to generate new sales. *(p.512)*

8. _____ A temporary price reduction offered by a manufacturer to stimulate sales. *(p.508)*

9. _____ Sales promotions that allow the customer to recover part of the product's cost from the manufacturer. *(p.508)*

10. _____ The use of the telephone or fax to sell directly to consumers and business consumers. *(p.511)*

11. _____ A discount to the retailer or wholesaler based on the volume of product ordered. *(p.506)*

12. _____ A salesperson whose primary function is to facilitate transactions that are initiated by the customer. *(p.512)*

13. _____ Communications strategies to build good relationships and corporate image with an organization's stakeholders, including consumers, stockholders, and legislators. *(p.499)*

14. _____ Unpaid communication about an organization appearing in the mass media. *(p.502)*

15. _____ A description of some event or news item that is sent to newspaper and magazine editors in the hope that it will be published as a news item. *(p.502)*

MULTIPLE CHOICE

Identify the most correct answer.

1. A person who has a high level of technical expertise and assists with product demonstrations is called a: *(p.512)*
   a. missionary salesperson.
   b. detailer.
   c. demo rep.
   d. technical specialist.

2. A promotion can be undertaken for many reasons, including the following: *(p.506)*
   a. Obtaining distribution or shelf space for a product.
   b. Decreasing the volume of product bought by a retailer.
   c. Creating lesser brand awareness among consumers.
   d. Discouraging consumers to try the product.

3. In general, promotions work best when: *(p.506)*
   a. they ruin relationships with retailers and wholesalers.
   b. they present a tangible benefit to the consumer, such as giving something away or stressing attractive and innovative product displays.
   c. long-term changes in market share are created.
   d. firms practice database marketing.

4. A sales follow-up includes: *(p.515)*
   a. data on past sales, testimonial of other buyers, and guarantees.
   b. developing information about prospective customers.
   c. setting outcome goals.
   d. sales activities which provide important services to customers after the sale.

5. A case allowance provides: *(p.506)*
   a. a direct payment to the retailer for stocking a product.
   b. a discount to the retailer based on the volume of the product ordered.
   c. reimbursement to the retailer for in-store support.
   d. payment to a salesperson every time he or she sells an item.

6. Incentive programs are promotions that: *(p.508)*
   a. allow manufacturers to show off their product lines to wholesalers and retailers.
   b. employ useful or decorative items imprinted with an organization's identification, message, or logo.
   c. recognize superior achievements, as when salespeople meet or exceed specific sales objectives.
   d. involve the consumer in the company's marketing efforts.

7. A high pressure sales technique is called: *(p.512)*
   a. a soft sell.
   b. a selling-formula.
   c. a relationship approach.
   d. a hard-sell.

8. Term(s) used to describe the awarding of discounts, bonuses or points is called a: *(p.510)*
   a. continuity program.
   b. membership program.
   c. loyalty program.
   d. all of the above.

9. The process of planning, implementing, and controlling the personal selling function of an organization is known as: *(p.515)*
   a. sales function.
   b. sales management.
   c. sales development.
   d. sales implementation.

10. Consumer promotion objectives are established to: *(p.506)*
    a. encourage decision-makers to select the item and stock it in larger quantities.
    b. build morale by demonstrating the level of support given to the product and by rewarding the salesforce for selling even more of it.
    c. feature an item prominently in retail advertising and on store shelves.
    d. stimulate impulse buying, reward loyal customers for continuing to buy the product, and to lure users of competing products away.

11. When two or more products or services combine forces to create interest using a single promotion tool, this is called: *(p.510)*
    a. cross-promotion.
    b. incentive-promotion.
    c. bonus-promotion.
    d. price deal.

12. The objective(s) of relationship selling include: *(p.512)*
    a. winning customers.
    b. keeping customers.
    c. developing customers.
    d. all of the above.

13. A set of customers, often defined by geographic boundaries, for whom a particular salesperson is responsible, is called a: *(p.516)*
    a. trade area
    b. central business district.
    c. sales territory.
    d. geodemographic.

14.   A public relations campaign plan should include the following element(s): *(p.502)*
      a.   A statement of the problem.
      b.   A marketing analysis.
      c.   A discussion of how the program will be evaluated.
      d.   All of the above.

15.   Interactive forms of public relations include: *(p.502)*
      a.   events.
      b.   ceremonies.
      c.   meetings.
      d.   all of the above.

CHAPTER IN REVIEW—WRITING TO LEARN

1.   Describe some of the advantages and disadvantages of sales promotions.

_____

_____

_____

_____

2.   Describe some of the various types of trade promotions frequently used by marketers.

_____

_____

_____

3.   Describe the steps in developing a public relations campaign.

_____

_____

_____

_____

CASE ANALYSIS

Real People, Real Decisions: Desiree Walsh and Tessa Vanderkop, Raincoast Books

Reread the three sections comprising the Raincoast Books vignette in Chapter 18 and answer the following questions:

1.   How did Raincoast Books spend the first part of its promotional budget for the launch of *Harry Potter and the Goblet of Fire*?

2.   What kind of publicity did the launch receive?

3.   What kind of awareness level did the launch of the new book achieve?

4.   What was Raincoast Books' objective for the *remainder* of its $200,000 promotional budget?

SCENARIO

Personal selling is an important component of the communications mix, and while it applies most often to the marketing of goods and services, personal selling also applies to many aspects of our lives. You, the student, will soon face a major challenge involving personal selling—selling yourself to an employer. In preparation for finding the position of your dreams, consider the following:

1.   Determine who your prospects are—those companies that you would like to work for. Do some research, identify companies and create a list of potential employers.
2.   Qualify your prospects—which have the most potential, which fit best with what you have to offer—based on your research?
3.   How might you plan a preapproach to a potential employer?
4.   You've had the interview—your "sales presentation". What do you do to followup?

ANSWERS

Chapter Outline

I.   ADVERTISING'S NOT THE ONLY GAME IN TOWN!—Three different promotional techniques can be used to make an impact; they are: public relations (free publicity), sales promotion (a focused campaign), and personal selling (delivering a sales pitch in person).

II.   PUBLIC RELATIONS—Communications strategies to build good relationships with an organization's stakeholders, including consumers, stockholders, and legislators.
        Publicity—Unpaid communication about an organization appearing in the mass media.
        A.   Objectives of Public Relations
                1.   Introducing new products.
                2.   Supporting current products.
                3.   Influencing government legislation.
                4.   Enhancing the image of an organization or entity.
                5.   Calling attention to a firm's involvement with the community.
                6.   Demonstrating social responsibility.
                7.   Developing positive employee or investor relations.
                8.   Handling communications issues and crises.
        B.   Planning a Public Relations Campaign
                1.   The organization must first develop clear objectives for the PR program that define the message it wants people to hear.
                2.   The PR specialist then creates a campaign strategy that includes: a statement of the problem, a situation analysis, specification of target audiences (publics), messages to be communicated, and specific program elements to be used, a timetable and budget, discussion of how the program will be evaluated.
                3.   Execution of the campaign means deciding how the message should be communicated to the stakeholder(s) of interest, for example, news conferences, sponsorship of charity events, or creating attention-getting promotions might be considered.
                        Press Release—Description of some event that an organization produces itself and send to the media in the hope that a reporter will write an article about it.

III.   SALES PROMOTIONS—A program designed to build interest in or encourage purchase of a product during a specified time period. Sale promotions focus on more short-term objectives.
        A.   Trade Promotions
                1.   Discounts and Deals—A manufacturer can reduce a channel partner's costs through sales promotions that give a discount on its own products.
                        Merchandise Allowance—Reimburses the retailer for in-store support of the product.
                        Case Allowance—A discount to the retailer or wholesaler based on the volume of product ordered.
                2.   Industry Boosting and Boasting
                        Trade Shows—Events at which many companies set up elaborate exhibits to show their products, give away samples, distribute product literature, and troll for new business contacts.
                        Promotional Products—Free products (i.e., coffee mugs, key chains, etc.) that are used to build awareness for the sponsor.
                        Incentive Programs—Designed to motivate a firm's own sales force.
                        Push Money—A bonus paid by a manufacturer to a salesperson for selling its product.

B. Consumer Promotions

1. Price-Based Consumer Promotions—Coupons, price deals, refunds, and rebates.

Rebates—Sales promotions that allow the customer to recover part of the product's cost from the manufacturer.

Special Packs—A separate product given away along with another product.

2. Attention-Getting Consumer Promotions—Stimulate interest in and publicity for a company's products.

Contests and Sweepstakes—A contest is a test of skill and a sweepstakes is based on chance.

Premiums—An item included without charge when a consumer buys a product.

Sampling—Distributing trial-size versions of a product for free to encourage people to try it.

Point-of-Purchase (POP) Promotion—The use of signs or displays to influence purchases at the store level.

Loyalty-Generating Promotion—Continuity programs, membership programs and loyalty programs targeted to frequent and high-value customers.

Cross-Promotion—Two or more products or services combine forces to create interest using a single promotional tool.

IV. PERSONAL SELLING—The part of the communications mix that involves direct contact between a company representative and a customer.

A. The Role of Personal Selling

Telemarketing—The use of the telephone or fax to sell directly to consumers and business customers.

Order Taker—A salesperson whose primary function is to facilitate transactions that the customer initiates.

Technical Specialist—Sales support personnel with a high level of technical expertise who assist in product demonstrations.

Missionary Salesperson—A salesperson who promotes the firm and tries to stimulate demand for a product but does not actually complete a sale.

Order Getter—A salesperson who works creatively to develop relationships with customers or to generate new sales.

B. Approaches to Personal Selling—The evolution from a transactional, hard-sell marketing approach to a relationship approach.

1. Transactional Marketing: Putting on the Hard Sell

Transactional Selling—A form of personal selling that focuses on making an immediate sale with little or not attempt to develop a relationship with the customer.

2. Relationship Selling: Countering the Tarnished Image

Relationship Selling—A form of personal selling in which the salesperson seeks to develop a mutually satisfying relationship with the consumer so as to work together to satisfy each other's needs.

C. The Role of Personal Selling in the Communications Mix—The salesperson's job can be made easier with support from publicity and advertising.

D. The Selling Process—The series of activities necessary to bring about a transaction.

Creative Selling Process—The process of seeking out customers, analyzing needs, determining how product attributes might provide benefits for the customer, and then communicating that information.

1. Prospect Customers

Prospecting—A part of the selling process that includes identifying and developing a list of potential or prospective customers.

2. Qualify Prospects—A part of the selling process that determines how likely prospects are to become customers.

3. Do a Preapproach—A part of the selling process that includes developing information about prospective customers and planning the sales interview.

4. Make the Approach—The first step of the actual sales presentation in which the salesperson tries to learn more about the customer's needs, create a good impression, and build rapport.

5. Make the Sales Presentation—The part of the selling process in which the salesperson seeks to persuasively communicate the product's features and the benefits it will provide after the sale.

6. Overcome Customer Objections—Reasons why the prospect is unwilling to commit to a purchase, and the salesperson is prepared to overcome objections by providing additional information or persuasive arguments.

7. Close the Sale—The stage of the selling process in which the salesperson actually asks the customer to buy the product.

8. Follow-up After the Sale—Sales activities that provide important services to the customers.

E. Sales Management—The process of planning, implementing, and controlling the personal selling function of an organization.

1. Setting Sales Force Objectives—What the sales force is expected to accomplish and when.

2. Creating a Sales Force Strategy—How the firm will structure, determine the size, and compensate its sales force.

Sales Territory—A set of customers often defined by geographic boundaries, for whom a particular salesperson is responsible.

3. Recruiting, Training, and Rewarding Salespeople

Recruiting—Attracting and hiring the right set of people to do the job is a top priority for sales managers.

Sales Training—Allows salespeople to learn about the organization and its products and to develop selling skills.

Rewarding Salespeople—Common payment systems used to motivate salespeople include: a straight commission plan, a commission-with-draw plan, and a quota-bonus plan.

Key Terms

1. Sales promotions
2. Merchandise allowance
3. Qualify prospects
4. Premiums
5. Point-of-purchase (POP)
6. Coupons
7. Order getter
8. Price deal
9. Rebate
10. Telemarketing
11. Case allowance
12. Order taker
13. Public relations
14. Publicity
15. Press release

Multiple Choice

1. d
2. a
3. b
4. d
5. b
6. c
7. a
8. d
9. b
10. d
11. a
12. d
13. c
14. a
15. d

Chapter in Review—Writing to Learn

1. Sales promotions assist marketing efforts by creating short-run changes in product sales, by cementing relationships with retailers and wholesalers, and by encouraging high levels of store traffic. Sales promotions also have some less attractive characteristics: they dilute brand equity, they teach consumers always to look for special offers, their effect is only temporary, and they often reach only current users.

2. Sales promotions aimed at industry members and retailers are called trade promotions. Sometimes trade promotions mean manufacturers work to help make retailers more successful by providing local advertising support, conducting sales training or giving the retailer a price allowance. Trade promotions aimed at sales forces and members of industries include trade shows where manufacturers can showcase their products for many buyers from around the country, specialty advertising, and incentive programs such as sales contests.

3. A public relations campaign begins with examining the current attitudes of various publics, determining the issues of interest, and then planning what action to take. A PR campaign may include sponsorship of an event, cause-related marketing activities, and/or developing print or video news releases about timely topics. As with other promotion tools, careful implementation and evaluation are important also.

Case Analysis

1. Raincoast Books spent the initial portion of its promotional budget on posters, bookmarks, stickers and party kits to support individual stores that planned special parties and other activities.

2. The launch received free coverage in all major cities in Canada, on TV and radio, and in magazines and newspapers.

3. Awareness levels for the launch of the new book were the highest of any book (or entertainment product, for that matter) ever released.

4. The main objectives for the latter part of the promotional budget were to direct the funds toward using author Rowling's time as efficiently as possible, and toward activities that would keep the momentum and sales going.